The People's Hist

The Town Of Old ...am

An Historical Miscellany In Words And Pictures

Edited by Keith Armstrong

The Civic Arms of Hexham.

Previous page: Hexham Market Cross and Fountain.

Copyright © Keith Armstong 2002

First published in 2002 by

The People's History Ltd
Suite 1
Byron House
Seaham Grange Business Park
Seaham
Co. Durham
SR7 0PY

ISBN 1 902527 69 0

Contents

The Town Of Old Hexham

A Parody on 'The Cliffs of Old Tynemouth'

The town of old Hexham, the pride of the Tyne,
'Midst beautiful landscapes and scenery so fine,
With Nature so bounteous in every degree,
So, the town of old Hexham for ever for me!

Chorus – So; the town, &c.

This old ancient town there is none can surpass,
For friendship, for flowers, for fruit, an' fair lass;
For hills, dells, and woodlands, and green mossy lea,
So, the town of old Hexham for ever for me!

Round the suburbs of Hexham, and along the whole strand,
There's grandeur depicted by Nature's fine hand,
With the rich fruits and flowers on each verdant tree,
So, the town of old Hexham for ever for me!

Yon lofty green hills, too, look pleasant and sweet,
With the prince of fine rivers that rolls at their feet,
And murmurs so sweet on his way to the sea,
So, the town of old Hexham for ever for me!

On its daisy-clad banks, too, delighted I've stood,
And gazed on its beauties of water and wood,
Where the notes of the blackbird sound loud from the tree,
So, the town of old Hexham for ever for me!

In thy sweet-scented by-lanes, so comely and sweet,
Decorated with verdure for lovers' retreat,
Where Venus and Hymen on terms can agree,
So, the town of old Hexham for ever for me!

O, then, for a wander through old Hexhamshire,
Where there's beauty and grandeur the poet to inspire;
Where the heather is laden with food for the bee,
So, the town of old Hexham for ever for me!

As I wander the Seal and the bonny Tyne Green,
The days of my childhood reflect on the scene,
Our mischievous pranks, more than one, two, or three,
So, the town of old Hexham for ever for me!

And long may old Hexham in beauty preside,
The fairest of places on bonny Tyneside;
And for neat, handsome lasses 'tween hero and the sea,
So, the town of old Hexham for ever for me!

James Anderson

Introduction

The market town of Hexham in Northumberland has an atmosphere all of its own. It is the product of a turbulent history which has seen the development of its beautiful Abbey, alongside the hard graft of its tradespeople, reflected in the glovemaking industry which produced the famous 'Hexham Tans', and the long suffering of its inhabitants through social turmoil in the shape of the notorious Riot of 1761, disasters, epidemics, and border insurgency.

This new 'People's History' book has been edited by Keith Armstrong of the 'Northern Voices' creative writing and community publishing project. It follows the success of his previous book on the Durham mining communities.

As a poet and community arts development worker, Armstrong draws together a unique selection of historical tracts, poetry, folk songs, historical documents, photographs and engravings, to bring Hexham's history to life. He builds on his own roots in Tynedale and develops the work he has already done on the town's history and community life reflected in the 'Hexham Celebration' for the 1992 Abbey Festival, his Year of the Artist 2000 poetry residency at Hexham Races, and successful performances, featuring locally inspired poetry and folk music, at the town's enterprising Queen's Hall Arts Centre.

The book has been produced with the close co-operation of local historians from the area who have kindly donated photographs and research material which make this unique volume all the more vivid. It makes no claims to be definitive – it is simply a tribute to the town and its people, a real people's history, and not the last volume we hope to publish on this passionate area of Northumberland.

Buses lined up in Beaumont Street in the early 1920s.

Acknowledgements

Thanks to local historians Tom Corfe (for his opening chapter and help with research) and Colin Dallison (for the loan of photographs from his collection and assistance with research).

Thanks also to Charles Enderby, Managing Director of Hexham Steeplechase Company, for access to historical photographs of Hexham Racecourse, and to photographer Tony Whittle for present day photographs of the Races.

The author would also like to thank Hexham Library and the Border Museum Library for help with research.

Some of the material in this book is the product of the 'Hexham Celebration', which the author devised for the 1992 Hexham Abbey Festival with the aid of Queen's Hall Arts Centre and Northern Arts, and of 'Hexham Tans', an informal show developed by the author and staged at Queen's Hall Arts Centre in 2000 (as part of the Northumberland Traditional Music Festival) and 2001, with the support of Northumberland County Council and Geoff Keys, Artistic Director at Queen's Hall.

Some of the written material on Hexham Races is the product of the author's poetry residency as part of Year of the Artist 2000 at Hexham Races which was supported by Northern Arts and Hexham Steeplechase Company.

Present day photographs of Hexham are by the author.

A postcard showing Hexham Hydro, now the Queen Elizabeth High School.

SECTION ONE

HEXHAM

THE HISTORY

BY TOM CORFE

Fore Street from the south a century ago.

It seems that there once lived in Northumbria a certain Hagustald. An important and powerful man, he was lord of a shire that stretched for eight miles north of the Tyne and nearly fourteen south, as far as the high moorland from which Tyne, Wear and Tees flow.

We know nothing of this Hagustald. We only know that when Hexham began, it was in a region called 'The Hagustald's Land' (or 'Island'), which was probably the later 'Hexhamshire'. Whoever he was, the Hagustald lived in the seventh century, in the earliest days of the Northumbrian kingdom and soon after the English came. In their language a hagustald was a young warrior of noble rank but with no inherited land. We cannot know for certain the identity of this particularly important Hagustald, but we can make a guess that he might have been the younger brother of St Oswald. Oswald was the king who rallied the Anglian Northumbrians around the Christian cross he set up at Heavenfield. They drove out the British invaders, and then Oswald invited St Aidan to spread the Christian faith among his pagan Northumbrian subjects.

When Oswald was slain in battle his brother Oswiu succeeded him, and perhaps brought with him the land that he had been earlier granted. Oswiu himself died in 670, and soon afterwards his daughter-in-law Etheldreda, the new queen of Northumbria, gave 'The Hagustald's Land' to Wilfrid, Bishop of the Northumbrians. Wilfrid needed this generous gift of land to support a monastery he planned to build.

Wilfrid was one of the great early champions of Christianity in England. In the heart of the Queen's estate he built a new church, a

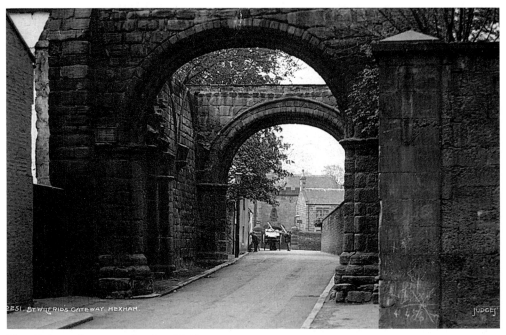

The Priory Gateway in the 1920s.

copy of the fine stone churches he had seen at Rome and in France. He chose a green terrace overlooking the Tyne; not far off was an ample supply of ready quarried stone, at the ruined Roman town of Coria – Corbridge. It is possible that some Dark Age chieftain had already built his hall on the terrace, or that Roman detachments had camped there, but of this there is no evidence. Before Wilfrid's church was built, we know only of prehistoric farmers living at the future site of Hexham.

'The Hagustaldian Church', as it was known, became under the dynamic guidance of Wilfrid and his successors a centre of faith and learning matching the other Northumbrian monasteries at Lindisfarne and Wearmouth-Jarrow. It also became a diocesan cathedral, an administrative centre from which Wilfrid and his successors exercised authority as far as the Tees. It was at the heart of Northumbria's Golden Age. Apart from the many fragments of richly carved stone, two remarkable survivals from the seventh century Hagustaldian Church underline its importance: the stone cathedra now called the 'frith stool' was the throne from which the bishops of Hexham ruled their diocese; and the crypt below the present nave was where relics of St Andrew were displayed to draw awestruck pilgrims to Wilfrid's church and the new faith it so proudly represented.

We do not know how many monks served Wilfrid's church, said to be the finest north of the Alps; though there may have been a hundred or more. They lived around it, in an assortment of wooden houses and halls spreading across the terrace, together with their lay assistants, craft workers and farm hands. Nothing survives from that monastic town. We can only guess at its nature from the excavated evidence of similar communities at places like Whithorn or Whitby.

In the ninth century, some 150 years after its foundation, Wilfrid's abbey faltered and decayed. It lost its bishop and ceased to be a cathedral. The community of scholar-monks dwindled and dispersed. They suffered from civil wars and perhaps from Viking raids. Someone carefully buried the monastic small change, some 9,000 bronze coins, in an old bronze bucket; but whoever it was never came back to recover it. It was a grave-digger who found the hoard in 1832. A family of hereditary priests kept the church and its memories alive through these difficult times, even patched the ageing building; but the small surviving community lived in an impoverished wilderness.

In the eleventh century the Normans arrived, and Norman bishops restored the English Church in a continental mould. Fresh ideas and new patterns of faith were emerging from France and Germany, and in 1113 the Norman Archbishop of York determined to revive the ancient glories of the Hagustaldian Church. He refounded it as a priory of Augustinian canons, a home for 26 priests who served in churches up and down the Tyne valley while living in a strictly ordered community. It was these canons who built, around and above the ruined remnants from Wilfrid's days, the great new church that has dominated the town centre ever since. The canons also surrounded their church and the buildings where they lived, worked and died, with a high stone wall.

Its entrance gatehouse still survives, though it has lost its roof and upper rooms.

Outside the priory wall grew a busy market town that soon acquired a name. Hextildesham, it was called, confusing the old 'hagustaldian' name with that of the Countess Hextilda, heiress of Tynedale, who used her wealth and royal connections for the benefit of the Priory. It was some centuries before 'Hextildesham' was abbreviated, in both written and spoken form, to the name we now use.

Hextildesham embraced several distinct communities, ecclesiastical and lay. The Priory was closely linked to the new feudal lords of the North. They, as well as the archbishops, gave widespread estates for the support of the canons; so the Priory became the centre of a large-scale landowning and farming enterprise. Moreover, as the safest and largest group of buildings on the east-west route along the Tyne valley and close to two main roads into Scotland, the Priory became a popular stopover for distinguished travellers. These included royal and papal messengers, ambassadors and their entourage, and on occasion both English and Scottish kings.

The Saxon Crypt in the Abbey.

The Night Stairs, Hexham Abbey.

The Frith Stool, Hexham Abbey. It is also known as the Bishop's Throne or the Sanctuary Seat.

A general view of the Abbey, around 1912.

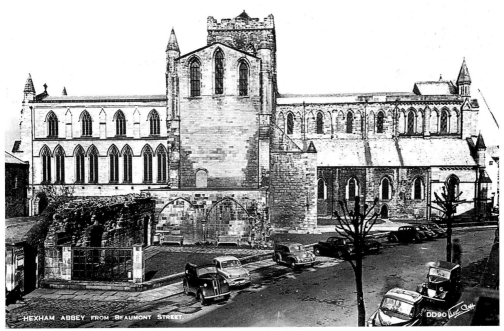

A postcard of the Abbey taken from Beaumont Street in the 1950s.

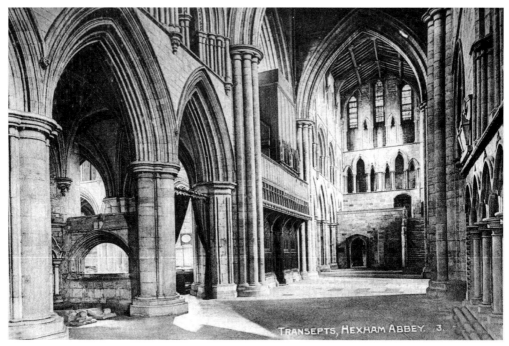

The Transepts of the Abbey.

The Saxon Apse – rediscovered when the floor was re-laid in 1908.

Prior Leschman's Shrine, South Transept. This postcard was sent to North Shields in 1906. The message reads: 'Enjoying ourselves a treat in Hexham.'

Hextildesham regained the administrative role once played by Wilfrid's church. Across the open market space outside the Priory wall was the Bailiff's Hall, a cluster of buildings overlooking the Tyne and its crossings from the north-eastern corner of the terrace. The Hall housed the local representative of the distant Archbishop of York, the Lord of Hexham. He held the former Hagustaldian Lands, which had become the Regality (or Liberty) of Hextildesham and were usually known as Hexhamshire. Here the Archbishop (or the Bailiff on his behalf) enjoyed complete authority, free of interference from the king's judges and officials, administering his own laws, taxes and justice. When the troubled times of the Scottish Wars brought poverty and unrest in the Archbishop's domains, he ordered the building of a strong prison tower at the Hall. Remarkably, it still stands. Later an even stronger gatehouse tower was added. It is now known as the Moot Hall.

Between and around these two substantial groups of buildings in their protected enclosures local farmers and travelling merchants exchanged wares in the open market space. Many built themselves stalls, houses or workshops on ground leased from the archbishop or the prior. By the fourteenth century the Lord of Coastley had built and leased out a row of cottages along the line of the later Fore Street.

Two postcard views of the east side of the Moot Hall in the early twentieth century.

The Market Place around 1905.

Around the area that came to be known as the Market Place there were other settlements, mainly concerned with farming the land but also housing rural industries like tanning, weaving and iron working. Such were Priestpopple, where the Priory had 24 tenants; Hencotes; and Cockshaw, where the burn waters were used by crafts and mills.

By the mid-thirteenth century the various ecclesiastical, administrative, commercial, agricultural and industrial communities formed a single Hextildesham, though its components retained separate identities as wards of the town and it never received borough status. Instead, the Bailiff exercised authority over both town and shire, backed by his entourage of receiver (who collected rents, dues and taxes), justices, constables and other officials. He presided over sworn juries of townsfolk and landholders who advised on all problems of local government. Exempt from interference by royal officials, and remote from their master in York, Bailiffs sometimes behaved arbitrarily and unfairly. There were occasions complaints, as when Roger de Saxton demanded a 'bailifpotte' duty from all who brewed their own ale, or William de Toluse accepted bribes for releasing thieves. William was also in trouble for seizing a fugitive criminal from Scottish territory and allowing his subsequent lynching. But the very survival of such complaints, and the steps taken to remedy the evils, suggest that most of the time Hexham folk lived in a well-ordered community.

Peace and prosperity came to a sudden end in 1296. Edward I asserted his rights as overlord of Scotland, and succeeded only in uniting and antagonising the Scots. In April a Scottish army swept down Redesdale bringing death and destruction. At Hexham they not only desecrated and fired the Priory, but burned the Priory School and 200 scholars within it. The atrocity was reported with horror and perhaps some exaggeration by English chroniclers. In the following year another Scottish force made its headquarters in the Priory. Its leader was William Wallace. His offer to respect the canons and their property was ignored by his ill-disciplined followers. The Priory had barely recovered from this burning and despoliation when Robert Bruce arrived in 1311 on the first of his devastating annual raids. The canons learned to submit to blackmail in exchange for peace, and though impoverished they gradually recovered. But the effect on the folk of Hextildesham was long lasting. The damage wrought by annual raiding armies and by bands of deserters from both armies was compounded by a series of unrelated difficulties, a disastrous cattle plague, an unprecedented sequence of cold and wet summers and the ultimate horror of the Black Death. Hexhamshire suffered from widespread distress, starvation and depopulation. The rural economy and the commerce upon which Priory and townspeople depended collapsed. It was an end to the time of growth for Hextildesham. Yet there seems to have been no fundamental changes. The Bailiff's government continued from behind stronger walls; markets were still held though perhaps on a reduced scale; while the canons took stock of their remaining properties and cut back on building plans, though they were able to add fine painted woodwork in the Choir.

The Middle Ages ended for Hexham in September of 1536, when a small group of royal officials arrived on a long-heralded visit. They were headed by Lionel Gray and Robert Collingwood, commissioners despatched by Henry VIII's minion Thomas Cromwell to enquire into the state of the Priory of Hexham. Marital and financial problems led the king both to suspect treasonable attitudes in such religious communities and to covet their accumulated wealth. The Reformation in the English Church, when royal authority replaced that of the pope, was one aspect of centralised administration under a London-based monarchy. The North had become a particular thorn in the royal side, impoverished and unruly as it was after centuries of Border conflict. Hexham's problems were typical of those that afflicted the region. Hexham men were liable to be called away to serve in the archbishop's private army or fight in his private wars against other Yorkshire magnates. The Bailiff, facing rent riots in 1515 and an attack on the gaol where he held complainants, responded by burning many homes. Hexham's market was reported to be infested by 80 to 100 'strong thieves' who robbed poor and gentle alike, taking their cattle, horses and corn and threatening to burn the homes of any who complained. Parliament complained that thieves and brigands took advantage of the Regality's independence to escape royal justice, and Henry VII himself had to apologise to the archbishop for seizing traitors who took refuge in the Shire. His son was made of sterner stuff, and set about restricting the power of provincial magnates like the Percy earls and over-mighty churchmen like the Archbishop of York. They were to be replaced by dutiful royal servants.

When Lionel and Robert rode into Hexham they met popular hostility. Hexham people resented outsiders, southerners, government officials, enemies of religion and of the Priory in particular. The great bell of the town was rung, and that of the Priory. The crowd that gathered was armed, the commissioners reported, with bills, halberds and other weapons of war. The company rode through the Market Place to the Priory precinct wall, and around it to the head of Gilesgate. There they found the Priory gates shut, while armed canons defied them from the gatehouse. They were forced to beat a retreat, but it was only a temporary defeat, and in little more than six months a royal army had closed the Priory for good and the canons were pensioned off. Reynold Carnaby of Halton, a loyal supporter of Henry VIII, took over management of the Priory and its estates, while the authority of the archbishop as lord of the manor soon after passed directly to the Crown. The former Regality was merged into the county of Northumberland. Thereafter, the families who became in turn lords of the manor, Fenwicks, Blacketts and Beaumonts, enjoyed only a fraction of the independent local authority once wielded by Bailiff and Prior.

Hexham no longer enjoyed importance as an administrative centre, and like the rest of northern England it suffered as a backward rural economy that had yet to come to terms with the lingering aftermath of warlike centuries. Visitors to the North like Lord Keeper North in 1676 and Celia Fiennes in 1698 felt they were venturing into a wilderness, the home of uncouth and primitive savages. Hexham had a particularly bad reputation as a haven for Papists at a time when they were widely seen as potential traitors. In fact, Catholics continued to play an active role as acceptable and responsible members of the local community. The industrial area outside the town centre where they were concentrated around their semi-secret mass houses became known as Holy Island. In the seventeenth century Hexham saw a good deal of religious upheaval, with such outspoken sects as the Quakers and Baptists loudly preaching their faiths. But the town remained safe from the impact of civil war and Scottish invasion, partly at least because the local roads were notoriously the most awful in the kingdom. It was more isolated and backward than at any time in its history.

The activities and preoccupations of Hexham residents in these centuries were reflected in the records of the manorial courts, especially the Borough Court which dealt with the petty problems of the town: rubbish dumping and pollution, unfair trading, minor property disputes or encroachment on the open fields, straying beasts, taking too much water from the public pant, occasional thieving, and (worst of crimes) harbouring Scotsmen. Into this self-contained world the county magistrates occasionally penetrated to hold quarter sessions in the Moot Hall, and to deal with the more serious matters of wider importance. If the county gentry did concern themselves about Hexham it was mainly to worry about Catholics, and twice in the earlier eighteenth century, in 1715 and 1745, they were particularly alarmed that Jacobite rebels might find ready local support. In fact Hexham played a negative role in the '45 Rebellion, for Marshal Wade's army, hastening from Newcastle to intercept the Scots at Carlisle, could get no further than the awful road beyond the town.

Apart from the passing unpleasantness of Jacobite rebellion, two episodes disturbed the rural tranquillity of eighteenth century Hexham. In March 1761, as popular unrest spread over plans to recruit by ballot for the part-time militia, working men from all over Tynedale converged on the town to mount a mass protest. The magistrates, meeting in the Moot Hall to conduct the ballot, feared insurrection and were ready for them. Six companies of the North Yorkshire Militia lined up in the Market Place to face the protesters, and when they eventually opened fire on the tight-packed crowd some fifty were killed. Ten years later natural disaster struck. The worst flood in memory struck the Tyne, sweeping away livestock, timber stacks, the crops and sometimes the homes of its market-gardening residents. It destroyed also the newly completed bridge across the Tyne that at last linked Hexham to a wider world.

The bridge was part of a transport revolution, which brought an end to this cosy, sluggish backwater existence. Earlier travellers had described with exasperation the hazards they faced to reach Hexham by riverside tracks, and the difficulties of crossing the Tyne anywhere else than at Corbridge. Wade's failure in 1745 was one stimulus to the

107.   TYNE BRIDGE, HEXHAM

The bridge at Hexham. It was built in 1793 after three earlier attempts had failed. The bridge was widened in 1967 by rebuilding the parapets so that they projected out to provide pedestrian footpaths.

spread of turnpikes, and before the end of the century good roads linked Hexham to east and west, as well as to the Northumberland coast at Alnmouth. The bridge that fell in 1771 was eventually replaced, though not until 1793 and only after two more failed attempts did the county bridge surveyors Robert Thompson and William Johnson finally succeed. About the same time, schemes to build cross-country canals linking Hexham to Tyneside fell through. But at last in 1838 the first of all cross-country railways finally joined Newcastle to Carlisle by way of Hexham.

At once what had been a wearisome and hazardous full day's journey for Celia Fiennes or Wade's soldiers became for Victorians a restful hour in a railway carriage. As a result it was possible for the market gardeners of Tyne Green to meet industrial Tyneside's demand for fresh fruit and vegetables, and for the wealthier commercial and professional citizens of Newcastle to enjoy rural homes.

Over the last two centuries Hexham has developed much like many other country towns. Its population has grown slowly, nothing like so rapidly as those of the industrial conurbations lower down the river. In 1800 just over one percent of the North-East's 320,000 people lived in Hexham. Now the town holds less than half of one percent of the region's two-and-a-half millions. But the vast change in living style and standards means that a tripled population now occupies a sprawling area more than twenty times as large as the town of 1800. Until the 1890s, growing numbers crammed into existing town centre housing; thereafter new estates spread outwards with ever increasing momentum until after the Second World War the detached and the semi overwhelmed the surrounding green hills. As local and rural industries shrank away, an increasing proportion of this population was either retired or employed away from the town. Weaving, tanning, glovemaking and other local industries vanished, to be replaced by supermarkets, by multifarious small business units clustered into featureless industrial estates, and by a vast and unsightly woodchip factory.

Growth brought problems, and problems brought reform.

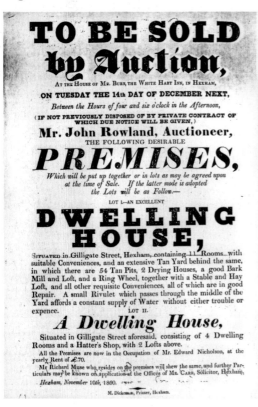

A notice advertising the auction of dwelling houses.

What happened in every country town across the kingdom happened also in Hexham. Mid-nineteenth century concern over public health led in 1853 to a damning official report, and that eventually brought an elected Board of Health, piped water supplies, sewerage, a cemetery, public lighting, new streets and slum clearance. National concern over educational standards produced, in Hexham as elsewhere, a School Board and eventually an integrated hierarchy of schools. Problems of faith and doubt led first to an explosion of denominational chapels and

The new Queen Elizabeth Grammar School opened in 1910.

A class dressed for a pageant at the Grammar School.

then, in the later twentieth century, their equally rapid disappearance. Poverty and social distress was handled first by a Board of Guardians which built a Workhouse with its hospital and school, and later by a District Council Social Services department. The demand for leisure amenities was met partly by public and partly by private enterprise, bringing parks and sports facilities, a theatre, cinemas, libraries, clubs and institutes. All these amenities helped in the growth of a lively and educated local community, well described in the memoirs of Joseph Parker, the Congregationalist leader who grew up in Hexham, and William Robb, who lived in it throughout his life.

The patterns of life in a Northern country town have changed over the past two centuries. Local has given way to national and universal; isolation and individuality have been replaced by the common culture and preoccupations of the modern world. In the steady erosion of separate identity, the relics and memories of a rich past remain Hexham's most distinctive and valuable asset.

Robert Bolam Short (1842-1930) in Beaumont Street in the late nineteenth century. He was hired as a farm worker at fourteen years of age and worked for 40 years as a rolley man – a carter – at the railway station. In 1864 he led the first load of stone from Oakwood Quarry for the Town Hall. In 1892 he was elected as the workingmen's rep on the Board of Health. Three years later he was elected to the newly set up Urban District Council. Between 1910 and 1928 he was a representative on the Board of Guardians for the Workhouse. A member of Hexham Wesleyan Society, he was a church officer and also a member of the Oddfellows and the Ancient Order of Forresters.

THE 18TH CENTURY

The Shambles, Market Place. This was provided for market traders by the Lord of the Manor, Sir Walter Blackett, in 1766.

James Wilson, from *Rhymes of Northern Bards* (ed John Bell Jnr, 1812)

The Banks Of Tyne

Apollo, your aid I request,
Direct and embellish each line;
With influence warm my breast,
To sing the sweet Banks of the Tyne.

If Phoebus proposes the theme,
Both reason and duty combine,
To pay my respects to the stream,
And honour the Banks of the Tyne.

How oft with great pleasure I stray,
Nor ever find cause to repine,
While Nature's rich beauties display
Themselves on the Banks of the Tyne.

Here Liberty's pleased to resort,
Her banners with lustre here shine;
No place, since she left the vile court,
Can please like the Banks of the Tyne.

Her sons are with Liberty fir'd,
Their Freedom they'll never resign;
But what their forefathers acquir'd,
Defend on the Banks of the Tyne.

The man let me freely explain,
Who would as a senator shine,
'Tis THERON, who holds his domain,
Enclos'd by the Banks of the Tyne.

Hexham seen from across the Tyne.

The following lines, written on laying the Foundation stone of Hexham Bridge, the author had the Honour to read at the Head of the Table, at the sumptuous Entertainment given by Sir Walter Blackett, on the occasion.

Unsullied mirth attend this feast,
Let joy shine forth in every guest,
And ev'ry face look gay;
Let not a cloud depress the scene,
But all look cheerful and serene,
'Tis our rejoicing day.

Come, Joy, with all thy smiling train,
Here take thy rest, securely reign,
See Phoebus shines more bright,
Here will we this great day adorn,
Till Cynthea with her silver horn,
Illuminates the night.

A bridge o'er Tyne! our joy's complete,
With rapture we its author greet,
Our breasts exult and sing;
This bliss consummates all our care.
Now Hexham and Elysium are,
But two words for one thing.

James Wilson

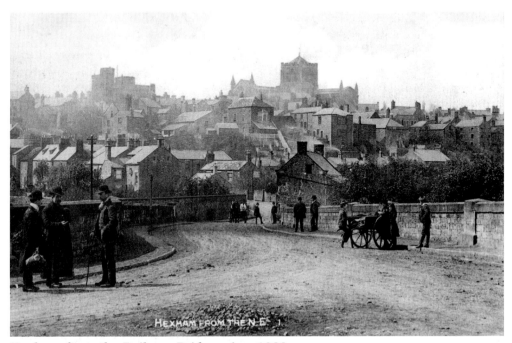

Hexham from the Railway Bridge, *circa* 1900.

A View of Northumberland, 1776

by W. Hutchinson

As we approached Hexham the prospect opened upon us in a beautiful manner; the cultivated vale was painted with all the happy assemblage of woods, meadows and corn lands; through which flows the Tyne ... opposite to Hexham, on an eminence, stands the church of St John Lee; beneath whose scite, the banks for near a mile, are laid out in agreeable walks, formed in a happy taste, appertaining to the mansion of the Jurin family; a modern building, seated at the foot of the descent, and fronting towards Hexham; having a rich lawn of meads between it and the river. This place is called the Hermitage; ... From hence the vale extends itself in Breadth, and is terminated with the town of Corbridge: the hills which arise gradually from the plain, on every hand are well cultivated, and own the seats of many distinguished families. Over this pleasing scene, Hexham, from an eminence, looks like a gracious Princess on their opulence of her dependants, rejoicing in their prosperity and peace.

Hexham is a place of great antiquity; Bede called it Hangustald; by the old English Saxons it was named Hextoldesham; and some authors (particularly Camden) say it is the Axelodunum of the Romans, that name implying its high situation, by the application of the old British name Dunum, a hill, by Hextol, a little rivulet so called, which washes its western foot ...

The remains of this ancient cathedral bear innumerable marks of magnificence. Many ancient tombs are here: within the quire is the recumbent effigy of an Ecclesiastic hooded, on a table monument of black marble, in relief; at the foot, a shield with ... an emblematical device to denote mortality, being the resemblance of cross bones. The people who keep the doors, say it is the tomb of Prior Richard, an Historian of the 12th century ... The device on the shield ... will then appear to be the letter *r i* placed one over the other ...

Mr Gale and Dr Stukeley, in the year 1726, visited the vaults of this church, now used as a private burial-place. What will not Curiosity attempt! ... Our curiosity urged us, at a distance of 49 years after those learned visitors had inspected the vaults, to see the antiquities they mention: perhaps they had entered into open cells, then unused for sepulture: our descent was more solemn. These vaults have for several years past been used as a private burial-place, and the entrance is covered with a table of marble, of prodigious size, which is not usually moved but at the denunciation of mortality. The massive Claustrum was heaved from the mouth of the vault by iron crows and rollers, at which the ground trembled over the arches – by a ladder we descended about 20 feet, into the regions of the dead, where avaricious curiosity making an anxious research after the objects of its desire, so compleatly occupied the mind, that scarce one reflection was agitated, for those, over whose ashes we wantonly trampled ...

At the west end of the church are the remains of the Priory. It was a spacious building, with an adjoining cloister. The refectory is yet entire, and serves as a room of entertainment at public times; it is very spacious, with a roof of oak work ...

This place is not very populous, the inhabitants being computed at 2,000 souls: the streets are narrow, and ill built. The Market-place, near the centre of the town, is a spacious square; in which is a convenient piazza for the butcher-meat, the stalls being moveable. The town is supplied by a fluent fountain of water, in the Market-place. Two markets are held here in the week, on Thursday and Saturday; and there are two annual fairs.

Leading to the Priory, is a gate-way of very ancient architecture; the arches form a semi-circle, and are moulded in a stile which denoted their antiquity to be much greater than any part of the Priory or cathedral ... The roof of the gate-way is of ribbed arching, meeting in the centre; the interstices, filled with thin stones or bricks, such as are seen in Roman works. The passage is divided into a large gate-way for horsemen or carriages, and a narrow one for foot passengers. The superstructure is in ruins ...

There are two ancient towers in the town, the one used as a Court or Sessions-house, anciently an exploratory tower, belonging to the Bishops and Priors of Hexham; the other situated on the top of the hill towards the Tyne, of remarkable architecture; being square, containing very small apertures to admit the light, and having a course of corbels projecting a long way from the top, which seem to have supported a hanging gallery, and bespeak the tower, at present, not near its original

The Night Stairs.

height ... This last-mentioned tower, having two dreadful dungeons within it, doubtless has been the chief fortress of the place, and was used as a prison when the Bishops of Hexham possessed their palatine jurisdiction ...

This town is not incorporated, but being a manor of the late Sir Walter C. Blackett, is governed by a Bailiff and Jury.

Hexham has been unhappy in civil bloodshed; the slaughter made by the North-Riding Yorkshire Militia on the Miners, in their insurrection, is remembered with horror. No troops in the world could have stood with greater steadiness and military propriety than they did, sustaining the insults of an enraged crew of subterranean Savages; whilst the tim'rous Magistrates delayed their command for defence, till the arms of the Soldiers were seized by the Insurgents, and turned on themselves; and an Officer was shot at the head of his Company, as he was remonstrating to the Mob.

Hexham is conveniently situated, for a traveller to make his excursions over the neighbouring parts of the county: the accommodations are excellent.

Mass House (with a priest's hole). Above the door is a date: '1657'. The house on the right is dated 1737.

THE HEXHAM RIOT, 1761

A crowded Market Place at Hexham in the 1920s. In 1761 a crowded Market Place was the scene of tragedy.

The Hexham Riot, otherwise known as the Hexham Massacre or the 'Late Dangerous Insurrection', was the most serious civil disturbance in Britain between the Edinburgh Riot of 1736 (with far fewer casualties) and the London Riots of 1780 (with many more). Yet it is forgotten by history, and it has no memorial in Hexham. Fifty-one people died in Hexham Market Place on 9th March 1761, during a futile protest against the Militia Laws. Next day's rain washed the cobbles clean of their blood, while establishment monopoly of the media blotted out any record of their tragedy.

Lack of a popular press and of any democratic process made rioting the only way for the lower orders to express dissent. Lack of a police force made it inevitable that criminal elements would take advantage of such rioting. To deal with such dangerous manifestations of popular unrest an efficient militia was needed, part-time soldiers to support law and authority. The militia would also back up the army in case of foreign invasion, for war had raged with France since 1756. Under the 1757 Militia Act each lord lieutenant appointed deputies to recruit part-time soldiers: the landowning gentry to serve as officers, the rank and file to be raised by ballot from workers in industry and on the land. These men would complete twenty days annual training for three years of service. They would not be sent overseas, and would serve only in emergency; so they were assured, though few of them believed the assurances. At Hexham, the Yorkshire Militia, nearing the end of their three-year stint, faced Northumberland workers reluctant to be recruited in their stead.

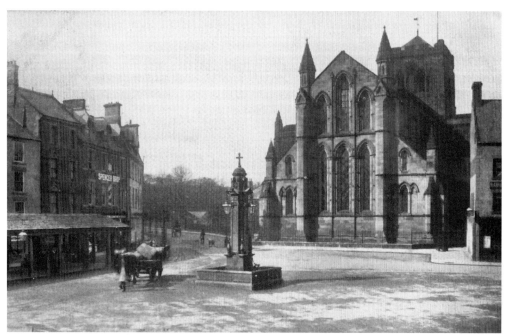

A more peaceful scene in the Market Place, one hundred and fifty years after the Hexham Riot.

There had been riots in 1757 and '58, and a troublemaker was hanged at York. Three years later the unrest began again. In the northern counties there was a widespread subversive movement, intended to frighten off the deputy-lieutenants and justices of the peace from enforcing the ballot arrangements. At Gateshead on February 28th it worked: the balloting was abandoned. At Morpeth on 2nd March it worked: a crowd armed with clubs, scythes and pistols beat and frightened the magistrates, and burned their lists. At Whittingham a day later it worked, and then at Etal and Belford. The leaders of the popular movement looked for similar success at Hexham, where the deputy-lieutenants were due to meet on 9th March to receive the new lists. But the authorities were ready to crush the movement.

The historical record tells the story from the establishment viewpoint. These are the words of a ruling class jealous of its rights and responsibilities, and alarmed by any challenge. The country gentlemen whose representatives met in the Hexham Moot Hall, the provincial press reporting their conduct, the militia officers anxious to justify their action (who might face criminal charges for unjustified killing) the clergy who reassured law-abiding citizens, the local authorities paying the busy surgeons and gaolers; all these were reacting against the threat of anarchy.

The common people who challenged authority, miners, rural workers and farm servants, have left no written record. Their arguments and attitudes can only be imagined.

Tom Corfe

From John Sykes, Local Records (1833)

1761: February 28th

The latter end of this month, a great deal of disturbance about the balloting for the militia took place in Northumberland and Durham. On the above day (Saturday), the mob having got a paper printed, came to Gateshead, in number about a thousand, and delivered it among the deputy-lieutenants, who were met to ballot for a few vacancies. The gentlemen, to avoid mischief, agreed to excuse them for that time at their expense (save a trifle from those on whom the lots fell), as only about a dozen were wanted in the ward. They then went peaceably home, but swore that they would stand to their proposal, as in their printed paper, whenever a general balloting happened again, and, at the same time begged his majesty might be petitioned to alter the Act. After the affair at Gateshead, the pitmen, waggonmen, husbandmen and servants in the county of Northumberland (for of such the mobs mostly consisted) having taken into their heads that the Durham people of their station had got exempt from the ballot by the rising that they had made, assembled on Monday, the 2nd of March, in great numbers, at Morpeth, and not meeting with such indulgence as they expected, obliged the deputy-lieutenants and justices to quit their duty for their own safety, no military force being at hand. The rioters then seized all the lists and books relative to the militia, from the constables, and tore or burned them before their eyes. The next day, they went to Whittingham, twenty miles up the country, and acted in much the same manner. Flushed with success, and reinforced to near five thousand, they made a similar attempt at Hexham, but had not the like success.

March 9th

The deputy-lieutenants met at Hexham, pursuant to advertisement, to receive lists from the constables, of the persons in Tindale ward liable to serve in the militia; and being previously informed from several parts of the county, that a great number of persons were determined to assemble in a riotous manner to prevent such lists being delivered in, a detachment from the two battalions of Yorkshire militia, quartered at Newcastle, was, at the request of the deputy-lieutenants and justices, ordered by Colonel Duncombe, under the command of Major Crowe, from thence to Hexham.

From the *Newcastle Courant* of 14th March 1761

We are informed by good Authority from Hexham that on Monday last the Deputy-lieutenants met there, pursuant to an Advertisement for that purpose, to receive Lists from the constables of the Persons in Tindale Ward liable to serve in the Militia.

A Detachment from the two Battalions of the Yorkshire Militia quartered at Newcastle, was ordered to Hexham; and on the Day of Meeting were drawn up in the Market-place, near to the Gate-way that leads to the Sessions-hall; and about Ten o'clock in the Forenoon, several Hundreds of Persons, armed with Clubs and other Weapons, assembled in a riotous Manner in the Market-place, and other streets adjoining. And though the Deputy-lieutenants and Justices received and heard in Court Petitions of several of them, which all tended to have the Militia Laws suspended, and not put in Execution; and did all that was in their Power to convince them of their Error, and induce them, and the Rest of the Rioters to disperse, yet they contemptuously continued together in the most daring and insolent Manner; repeatedly declaring, that if their Request was not granted, they would murder the Magistrates. Notwithstanding which, the greatest Lenity was shewn them; and the Militia continued under Arms upwards of four Hours. The Rioters still remaining obstinate and not dispersing, the Proclamation in the Act for preventing Tumults and riotous Assemblies was made; soon after which the Rioters attempted to force the Lines of Militia, to come at the Deputy-lieutenants; and one of them with a Pistol, wounded Ensign Hart, of which Wound he is since dead. A Party of the Rioters then breaking into the Militia, the Magistrates were obliged to, and did give the command to Fire, which was accordingly done; and a great many of the Rioters were killed, others of them wounded. This put a check to the Fury of the Rioters, who thereupon fled, and dispersed themselves.

The diary of William Allen, an officer in the North York Militia

(First published by Sir C. Sharp in 1824, later printed by Sykes)

Newcastle, March 7th

Received orders for two companies of each battalion to march early to-morrow morning for Hexham, in order to put a stop to riotous assemblies intended to be held there on Monday to obstruct the deputy-lieutenants ballotting for the militia.

Sunday, 8th

Arrived safe at Hexham, at ten – found the people all resolute, and determined to rise, from a notion that those who assembled at Newcastle had their grievances redressed. Sir Rt Bewick, Sir Lancelot Allgood, Fenwick, &c, &c, supped with us.

Monday, 9th

At nine, were under arms – at ten marched to the town-hall with the justices – took possession of all the avenues leading to the hall, and drew up our men in the Market-place – Captain Fielding and his company were posted in the yard. The gentlemen proceeded to business, and all the men who gave in their names and had petitions to present I conducted through the ranks, two at a time, and carried up to the gentlemen. The petitions they presented were of a treasonable nature, tending to obstruct the execution of the laws; and though they profess all duty and allegiance to the King, yet they declared, one and all, that they would not be ballotted for. The gentlemen told them that they would not dispense with the execution of the law, and though, however hard it might be, yet, as justices they were obliged to act under it as it then stood. Their numbers greatly encreased; and about twelve, two horns were blown, and every reinforcement they received was ushered in with loud huzzas. One of the men who blew the horns (at my instance) was apprehended, but the gentlemen thought proper to release him, after taking his name and place of abode. At one, they had increased to near 5,000, and greatly insulted our men, who for upwards of three hours bore it with the greatest coolness and moderation. At one, or a little after, the proclamation was read, and they (were) acquainted with the penalty they incurred if they did not disperse. They still continued waving their monstrous sticks, clubs, and quarter-staffs, in a most insolent manner over the heads of our men, for by this time they had come within reach of our bayonets, with which our front rank stood charged; and soon after (they) made a vigorous effort upon our left, and broke in upon them; one of the ringleaders seized a firelock of a man of Captain Blomberg's company, turned upon the man, and shot him dead upon the spot; at the same time Ensign Hart was shot by a pistol from one of the mob, upon which the word of command was given to fire, as it then became an act of necessity and self-defence. The men were immediately formed again, and the fire became general from right to left. The grenadiers fired but once, which cleared our front, and in a minutes time there was scarce a man left but the dead and wounded. As soon as ever the smoke of the first fire cleared away, and I saw the resistance had ceased, I ran up and down the line to make the men give over firing – for many random shots continued, and the balls whistled by me both on right and left, but providentially I received not the least harm. Thanks be to heaven, my endeavours met with immediate success, and I found Major Crowe and Captain Hill employed upon the same business; and now we had an opportunity of contemplating the bloody scene before us, twenty-four being left upon the spot, eighteen of whom were dead and the rest dangerously wounded. This was a spectacle that hurt humanity, for now all resistance was over, compassion took place. We seized upon all their clubs, but took no prisoners, because the gentlemen chose to have them apprehended in a regular way by afterwards issuing their peace-warrants. Everything was now at an end. Col Duncombe's detachment had one officer mortally wounded, one private killed upon the spot, and three wounded. The man who shot Ensign Hart was instantly despatched, as was the other man who killed the soldier. We had not so much as a single officer or soldier hurt; owing, I apprehend, to the care Captain Revely and I took in keeping our front clear, for whenever they attempted to press upon us, we made our men charge their bayonets, and Revely and I advanced with ours at the same time, and made them give way. Finding no impression was to be made there, they altered their plan and made their attack as before-mentioned, which was foolish and desperate to the last degree. Our men behaved with the greatest steadiness that troops could possibly do, and the officers with a resolution that showed they were not backward in obeying their orders.

At four, marched our men to the abbey, and lodged them altogether in the great old hall.

At eight, went to see poor Hart; found him resigned and quite sensible, and spoke very cheerfully, but said he could not continue long.

Tuesday, 10th

Ensign Hart died this morning at five. No disturbance at all; a very wet day, which was of service, as it washed the remains of yesterday out of the Market-place. At six, all the officers and gentlemen attended the funeral of Ensign Hart – the officers supported the pall – the men marched with reversed arms and the drums beat the dead march, and every honour was paid him, except the firing, which was omitted, lest it should give umbrage to those who had lost friends in the affair, as many people were now come to town to challenge the dead and wounded. Buried the soldier at the same time. Fourteen of the rioters buried tonight, and others carried home, and some remained unowned. – All quiet.

List of those who were killed or died from wounds; taken mainly from 'An Account of the Dead and Wounded in the Hexham Riot', from the diary of Francis Armstrong, attorney of Hexham.

Soldiers:

Joseph Hart.
David Greenock.

Hexham:

Sarah Carter, with child.
Thomas Levestone's wife, with child.
John Dodd, shoemaker.
David Turnbull, labourer.
Thomas Usher, servant, Delegate Hall.
David Marrow, labourer.
Christopher Johnson, son of Robert Johnson.
John Armstrong of New House, Hexhamshire.

Slaley parish:

Matthew Carr.   Michael Burdess.
James Robson's son.   Andrew Lamb.
Matthew Fairlamb, Crinkley, farmer.

Broomley:

Henry Leighton, tailor.   Robert Brown, servant.

Corbridge:

Ralph Shotton.   Thomas Richardson.

Bywell parish and Whittonstall:

– Brown.   – Brown, his son.
Humphrey Brown, his son.

Prudhoe:

– Heslop, pitman.

Simonburn:

John Mintaff.   James Young.

Blanchland:

George Siddle of Crook Oak.

Newburn:

William Crow, weaver.

Fourstones and Newburgh:

William Watson.   Henry Hoggart, pitman.

Haydon Bridge:

Nicholas Forster of Staward.

Hollings in Derwentside:

Mr Thomas Forster.

Ryal Town:

Henry Dun, son of Richard Dun.

Throckley:

William Rotherford.
– Pescott of Heddon on the Wall.
John Cutter of Heddon on the Wall.

Chollerton:

Jacob Coulson, Gunnerton.
John Charlton, Birtley.
William Hepple, Birtley.
Thomas Dodd.
William Scott of Swinburn.

St John Lee:

Thomas English, Anick, labourer.
Anthony Brown, Sandhoe.
George Johnson, Wall.

Stamfordham:

Joseph Dodd.   John Proud.
John Elliot.   John Appleby.
Thomas Hudspeth.

Hartburn:

John Row.

Walwick:

Thomas Forster.

Kirkheaton:

Robert Atkinson.

49 Civilians – 2 Soldiers.

THE 19TH CENTURY

An illustration of the Market Place from around 1820 showing the White Horse Inn.

Mary Russell Mitford, letter to her mother, 1806

Little Harle Tower,
Nov 2, 1806

To Mrs Mitford,
Bertram House

The promising appearance of yesterday morning, my dearest mamma, tempted us to set forward on our expedition to Hexham. On our arrival we drove immediately to the abbey, where Colonel Beaumont had arrived only the night before. The colonel was delighted to see us, and pressed us much to stay for dinner. This we of course refused, as it was rather too much to travel twenty miles after a six o'clock dinner. We, however, accepted his offer of seeing the beautiful church, which joins his house; and Lady Charles took me to see the abbey itself. Upon repairing and beautifying this house, in which they only spend about a month in the year, the poor colonel has lately expended upwards of twelve thousand pounds. It was a fine specimen of the Saxon-Gothic architecture; but he has built upon the same foundation, retained all the inconveniences of the ancient style, and lost all its grandeur. It has on the outside an appearance of a manufactory, and the inside conveys the exact idea of an inn. I should have thought it absolutely impossible to construct so bad a house with so many rooms. There is but one good one, which is the ball room, and this is made the passage to the bed chambers ...

Hexham from Windmill Hill, *circa* 1830.

In order to render the bad taste of this abominable modern house still more conspicuous, it is contrasted with the singular beauty of the adjoining cathedral, whose gloomy magnificence and fine pointed arches delighted me extremely. The colonel is the patron, I may almost say the proprietor, of this fine church (for he is what they call a lay bishop, and still receives the tributary pence from the communicants), yet that part of the edifice where the pews are placed is in a most shocking state. The bottom of one of the pews, situated exactly under his own, is covered with straw like a London hackney coach; and even his own pew seems quietly resigned to the moths and other depredators. Everything, in short, seemed to testify it was a place he seldom visited.

We dined at a very wretched inn, for I must confess, in spite of the prepossession I felt in favour of my dear Ittey's* native town, that Hexham is a shocking gloomy place. After dinner I had the pleasure of visiting the house where my darling was born. It has been an extremely good one, and still retains a very respectable appearance; but it is now divided, and on one side of the street door, which still remains, is a collar maker's shop, and on the other a milliner's. We entered the latter, and purchased three pair of Hexham gloves, one for papa, one for my dearest mamma, and one for Ammy. I thought that, both as a memorial of the town and of the house, you would like that better than any other trifle I could procure.

* Her father, George Mitford (1761-1842), surgeon, who moved to Alresford. His father, Francis (1722-68), uncle George (1726-1811), and grandfather George (1694-1750) had all practised as surgeons.

An illustration of the old Market Place, 1810.

History of Hexham, 1823

by A.B. Wright

According to the census of June 1821, the number of houses in the township of Hexham was as follows:

Inhabited Houses,	513
Uninhabited Houses,	12
Houses then in building,	4
Total	529

From an accurate statement, in which the houses of the township not immediately in the vicinity are omitted, we find the numbers

In Market-street Ward,	128
Hencotes Ward,	65
Gilligate Ward,	83
Priest-popple Ward,	121
Suburban,	70
Total	467

According to another division, there are 83 cottages and 446 assessed houses, giving a total of 529 to the township.

Mr Hutchinson passed through Hexham in 1743-4, and estimated the number of inhabitants at 2,000 persons. In 1801, the township contained 3,427 persons; of whom 1,500 were males and 1,927 females. In 1810 the town alone contained 1,397 males, 1,855 females, and 873 children under 12 years of age.

In 1811 the census gives 3,473 persons, and the returns for 1818 are said to be mere copies of those of 1811. For 1821 the returns afford the following information.

Number of families,	1,030
Males,	1,805
Females,	2,319
Total	4,124

Of these, 615 families were employed in trade, 149 in agriculture, and 266 not employed in either of these pursuits. The population at present is supposed to amount to 5,436.

From these details a progressive improvement is made evident and it is probable that Hexham never was so populous as at present.

The dressing and manufacture of leather have long been the staple trade of Hexham. It is not easy to point out the period of its introduction. The name *Skinner Burn* has been applied to *Bondgate* since the date of Mr Wallis's History, as may be inferred from his using the latter name. Old inhabitants remember its entire occupation by the artizans whose designation it now bears. Old tombstones in the churchyard of Hexham and in the burying ground at Swallowship, now destroyed, bear the insignia of the glover. But none of these claim a high antiquity for the leather trade of Hexham; and the earliest writers who mention the subject only say in general that it has been '*long* celebrated for its manufacture of leather.' The trade has seldom been more flourishing than at present. The following table will show the extent to which it is now carried on:

Men and Boys employed as Leather-dressers and Glove-cutters,	71
Boys employed as Dusters,	40
Women in Hexham and its vicinity employed as Sewers,	1,000
Total	1,111

Raw skins used annually,	80,000
Skins of dressed Leather imported annually,	18,000
Total	98,000

A crowd of Hexham folk gather in the shadow of the
Abbey from an illustration drawn in the 1830s.

There are annually made and exported 23,504 dozens of pairs of gloves.

The quantity of Dutch Oker used is about 5 tons annually. 'An argillaceous pale yellow earth, mixed with white and spangled with flat talcy particles, is found at High-sheel, near Hexham, and is useful to glovers.' This is called by the workmen *fell clay*, but, being of an inferior quality, is seldom and little used. During the war with Holland, however, when the proscription of trade prevented the importation of Dutch Oker, the fell clay was almost wholly used, and was found to serve the purpose.

The second important branch of the leather trade is *Tanning*, which is carried on to a considerable extent. There are four tanneries; the number of men employed does not exceed 18, and that number dressed in the course of last year 5,000 hides and 12,000 calf skins. The tanneries of Messrs Carr and Dodd are distinct from the glove trade.

The art of making stuff *Hats* appears to have been introduced into Hexham soon after the discovery of the art itself. There are sixteen master hatters. To recite the names of all would be tedious, and to make distinctions would be improper and invidious. The number of persons employed differs with the season; during the summer months 35 or 40 have been at work, while the winter establishment rarely reaches 20. This is nevertheless an important branch of the trade of Hexham.

There are two *Woollen Manufactories* in the hands of Messrs. W. and H. Hart. These are principally employed in the carding and dressing of wool for the consumption of the neighbourhood. In both the machinery is worked by steam. The engines are cylindrical, acting by compression, and of about 4 horses' power. This branch of trade employs about 20 persons, and its management is said to do credit to the directors.

There are 38 *Looms* for the manufacture of Linen, Cotton, &c. in constant employ, but no extensive establishment. There are two Rope manufactories in a flourishing condition under the management of Messrs Bamburgh and Busby. One very considerable *Brewery,* the property of Mr Armstrong, is situated in Priest-popple; and another of yet greater magnitude, which, though not immediately within the limits of our subject, is important to it; this is Mr Elstobb's Brewery on the north side of Tyne Bridge, about a furlong distant from Hexham, and in the parish of St John Lee.

A water Corn-mill of complicated machinery and extensive power is situated on the bank of the river, beneath the bridge. It is conducted by Mr Dixon, and called Tyne Mills. A little higher up the river on Tyne Green, stands a Wind-mill still in use, and the ruins of a similar erection, but of earlier date, crown the Windmill Hill, on the west side of the *Seal*.

There are in Hexham thirty-two Inns and Public-houses. The principal are the Black Bull, a very old house that seems to have given a name to the Bull Bank on which it stands, and the White Hart, situated in the angle between Fore Street and the head of Priest-popple, most conveniently for the Mail coach and other carriages on the road between Newcastle and Carlisle. At the Black Bull (Mrs Thomsons) the Excise Office is held, here too is the Assembly Room, and the True Briton coach stops here on its way from Newcastle to Carlisle; it starts at 7 in the morning from Dixon's, White Hart, Old Flesh-market, Newcastle, and arrives at Hexham at 10 am and returns next day at 2 pm on the way from Carlisle. The Mail arrives at the White Hart, Mr Burn's, at half-past 10 am remains 20 minutes, and then starts for Carlisle. The Mail from the latter place arrives at half-past 3 on its way to Newcastle. A stage-coach, called the British Queen, starts daily (Sundays excepted) at 8 am. It reaches Newcastle at noon, and returns between 8 and 9 in the evening of the same day to Mrs Charlton's, Gray Bull Inn, Battle Hill, whence it departed.

In addition to these conveniences for trade, a commodious Gig has been lately established to run on the south side of the Tyne. It is called the Traveller, starts from Hexham at 7 in the morning, and returns late the same evening.

Messrs Watson and Erington, and other carriers, have carts every second day from Hexham to Newcastle. The carriers from Newcastle to Carlisle pass through Hexham at least twice a-week, viz on Monday and Wednesday. Carts from Brampton, Haltwhistle, Haydon-bridge, Alston, and Allondale, pass and repass twice a-week, and many thousand carts pass through from the lead mines to Newcastle. With these facilities it will be allowed that Hexham is well situated with respect to trade.

Four cows cross Battle Hill. Is that the farmer on the horse just behind them? This postcard was published by T&G Allan's, the well known stationers.

There are two annual Fairs at Hexham: the first for cattle, horses, swine, sheep, and lambs, altered from the 5th to the 6th of August: the other for fat and lean cattle, swine, and horses, altered from the 8th to the 9th of November. There are also two hirings for servants, at May-day and Martinmas. Tuesday is the weekly market-day, and there is an inferior market on Saturday.

The markets are extremely well supplied. Meat is as good, as cheap, in as great plenty, and at all times as easily to be procured, as in any town of the same size in England. Poultry, eggs, and butter, are cheap and in great plenty. Fish is scarce, and the want of water carriage is felt in this article. The distance from the sea and the land carriage contract the supply and injure the quality, while they increase the price. Vegetables do not hold a high place in the market, from the number of gardens, which enables almost every family to raise its own stock. Immense quantities of vegetables are sent from Hexham to the Newcastle markets.

Return of Grain annually sold in Hexham market.

Wheat, 4,000 quarters,	Oats, 2,000 quarters.
Barley, 1,000 ditto.	Rye, 1,500 ditto.

There is something peculiar in the measures which may be worthy of notice. Wheat and Rye: 2 Winchester bushels = 1 Hexham bushel. Oats and Barley : $2^{1/2}$ Winchester bushels = 1 Hexham bushel.

There are two Printing Offices in Hexham, where the work is distinguished for its neatness and accuracy. Messrs Dickenson and Barker are likewise proprietors of the two Circulating Libraries. There is

The Market Place around 1908.

The north side of Gilesgate before 1884.

no book-club, public subscription library, news-room, or reading-room, and we are sorry we cannot say that the encouragement afforded to the caterers for the mind's appetite reflects credit on the literary taste of the inhabitants of Hexham.

Without disputing the propriety of those laws which demand that the sick and needy shall be supported by their more fortunate brethren, we may be allowed to question the policy of that system which too frequently compels the upright and industrious to provide for the dissolute and the depraved. The poor of the township of Hexham are provided for, as usual, by rates levied occasionally, as circumstances demand. The established rate is 8d in the pound on the rental of land, and 6d in the pound on the rental of houses. The County or Constable Rates, amounting annually to £50, or £60, are paid out of the sums collected for the parish. The power of levying these rates is vested, as usual, in the discretion of a *select vestry*, who also regulate their appropriation.

In 1803 the rates for the whole parish of Hexham amounted to £2,001 2s 9¾d and for the township to £1,388 16s ½d at three shillings in the pound. But in 1810 the amount for the town only was £1,419 13s 7d, at four shillings in the pound.

The Poor-house is situated near the head of Priest-popple. It is a large irregular building and of different dates. Several poor families receive no farther relief from the parish than an asylum within these walls. The person presiding over the inmates is called 'the Master'. He contracts for the support of the establishment, and is responsible to the Overseers for the supply of necessaries and for the conduct of the persons committed to his trust. Each pauper admitted on the establishment is allowed by the parish two shillings and sixpence per week, paid to the master for his support. Other parishes or townships are allowed to join in the support of this establishment and to partake of its benefits. Such allies pay a sum not exceeding £2 2s yearly, besides the weekly pittance of 2s 6d for each pauper admitted on their behalf. In this league are many of the neighbouring townships, and it might be difficult to suggest a better or a cheaper mode of provision than is effected by such a union

The paupers' fare on Sunday and Thursday, which are called pot-days, is boiled beef, broth, and pease pudding, varied by other vegetables in season. Tuesday and Friday are collop-days, and afford fried bacon, &c. The savings of these days of plenty prevent the intervention of banian days in the Poor-house. In years of scarcity a thin starch-like mixture of flour and water made an occasional dish at the dinner table and constantly appeared at breakfast, but its place is now supplied by wholesome milk and nutritive crowdy. The more delicate dispose of their common viands to purchase an occasional dish of tea or some such luxury. The greatest attention is paid to cleanliness and order; and we strongly recommend to the unappetised *gourmand*, or the nice stomached lady of quality, an occasional peep into a poor-house, and cordially wish them a relish for paupers' fare …

The want of a resident magistrate, and the small power of the bailiff, may be supposed prejudicial to the interests of morality; yet few places can boast a greater absence of crime than Hexham. The lower class of people, even now, may be less civilized than their neighbours, although an amazing improvement has been wrought of late years. The preamble of an Act of Parliament, dated little more than two hundred years ago, sets forth, that in this district 'outrages were daily committed, black mail imposed, and persons carried away by violence and against their will.' The same Act makes all these crimes *felony*, and orders that the 'names of outlaws shall be proclaimed in the town of Hexham.'

And within the memory of persons now living an outrage was committed, which, whatever was its original motive, could only be disgraceful to the perpetrators; involving at once the character of the town and neighbourhood, confounding the innocent with the guilty, and imposing on the whole body a restraint and rigour, which, though evil in itself, has been the means of bringing forth much good; for now those degrading combinations are unknown, the laws are obeyed, not enforced; and experience and more enlarged ideas have changed the former warlike rudeness of the people of this district into a subdued but characteristic energy of manner, a respect for order and the constitution of their country, in one word, into patriotism – a rational love of freedom and the laws.

The present state of the streets in Hexham is not conducive to the health of the inhabitants. They are generally narrow, and one large house is often tenanted by several poor families. The pavement has been laid with little regard to the comfort or convenience of pedestrians, and lamps are scarcely known. The town is so situated that almost every street is formed on a descent, an advantage which might be made conducive to a state of greater cleanliness. The vicinity of the river, the general excellence of the roads, the bridge, and other advantages which will be alluded to hereafter, are favourable circumstances, of which the inhabitants do not sufficiently avail themselves.

The town is supplied with water from a considerable distance by two pants or common fountains. One of these was erected by subscription; and the other, from a Latin inscription on its front, appears to have been – *Presented to the Town by* ROBERT ALLGOOD, *Esquire, in the year 1703*. Water of a much superior quality is procured from a well on the west side of the Seal, of more real value than both the pants. These with the *burns* which pass through the town insure a plentiful supply of water; and to this circumstance and its salubrious situation, together with the invaluable privilege of exercise on the Seal, the inhabitants of Hexham owe that health and longevity which narrow streets and the neglect of cleanliness have not been able to counteract.

The Market Place.

Tyne Chylde: My Life and Teaching, 1830-1850
by Joseph Parker DD

Born, and born in quaint old Hexham, magnificent in antiquity, justly claiming to be a creation of Rome itself. That quaint town, rising in the quietness of old age over the silvery Tyne, witnessed the episcopal splendours of St Wilfrid, himself a true Northumbrian and the most famous Saxon prelate that ever invoked the Pontiff's protection. A town to be proud of, surely! A see, a manor, a county, twelve hundred years ago! There I was born in 1830, and there I lived for two-and-thirty years. I see it all now with closed eyes; its famed old abbey, its old-world Market-place, its ever-flowing pant, the ancient town hall of its own bishops and priors, its narrow streets, its environs of green undulations and sweet villages. I see the thriving tradesmen, the Mechanics' Institute where I borrowed my first books, the schoolmaster from whom I learned that all Gaul is divided into three parts, the other schoolmaster who punctuated his curt instructions with savage blows.

Birthplace! it must always be the town of towns to me; not that Eata was its first bishop, or that Tydferth was its last; not that in its monastery was the sacred frithstol, or stool of peace, or that in the time of the Edwards the privilege of Jura Regalia was conferred upon it; to me these are not so personally important as that an old house in the Market Place was one home, a house in Priestpopple another, and a third on the higher part of Battle Hill; there the strong father toiled at stone-cutting, and the patient mother gathered me often to her side in secret prayer …

Then, our academic kitchen! There not a few of the leading tradesmen would meet night by night, under the presidency of the solid and rubicund master, who ruled the proceedings with the baton of a long clay pipe. There was no little intelligence in that kitchen ecclesia, for the men of my native town in that day were readers and thinkers, and above all restless and eager disputants. To live was to argue, not to argue was to die. The subject was generally theological, and raged most fiercely around the ninth chapter of Romans, especially in reference to the cold and chilling figure of the potter and the clay. The smoking president was a strong Calvinist – and all the stronger for knowing nothing about Calvinism – whilst some of the smoking visitors were confirmed Arminians – not the less confirmed for not knowing whether Arminius was a shoemaker or a hymn-book. There was the well-read chemist, the sagacious carpenter, the long-headed jeweller, the learned wheelwright … I think I see now the smoky cloud and the glints of burning shag which accompanied those cheerful and positive conclusions; cheerful, because there was at least one kitchen-full of really saved people; and positive because ignorance cannot doubt. Ah me, how the panorama moves! On and on – the kitchen, the hot coffee, the emulous smokers, the fierce debaters, the sweet mother on the fringe of the assembly heartily wishing that Calvin had never been born, the boy sitting by the kitchen clock …

A visit to Hexham by rail, 1838

by Thomas Dibdin

A passenger secretly remarked to me: ' 'twas a bridal party, and the happy pair were to spend the day at Hexham.'

The word 'HEXHAM,' abstracted me a brief moment from all around, calling up recollections of former days in an instant; not only the more important events supplied by the pages of history, but of Colman's gratifying musical drama, called the *Battle of Hexham*; to which, in late boyhood, my eyes and my ears were riveted with a delight equally unqualified. The heroes who fought the real fight, and the heroes who represented it upon the stage – the author, the singers, the musicians – had all gone 'the way of dusty death.' In the midst of this abstraction, the train halted, and the ancient town of Hexham was close at my left. I shook myself, stepped out of the machine, reconnoitred our luggage, and concentrating it in a hand-truck, drawn by two steady lads, followed it up hill with my daughter into the heart of the town, stopping at 'the Bell,' the principal inn. From hence a chaise would convey us across the bridge to Great Chesters, a short six miles.

Here then was the capital of what was once called Hexhamshire. Here had been the seat of a bishopric, in ancient times. Here in fact (according to Pennant) was the *Hagustald* of Bede, and *Hextoldesham* of the Saxons. Here, the decisive battle was fought, which extinguished

A view of Hexham from the Railway Station.

the last hopes of Henry and Margaret driving them and their adherents as refugees out of the kingdom, and causing the latter to be visited, in retreat, by more misery and wretchedness than usually befall the lot of the vanquished. Here, the Reformation could not be consummated without fixing the head of the last Prior upon the gates of the abbey of which he was the principal.

It was market-day, and the population, consisting of some six thousand, seemed to be upon the *qui vive*. Of the market-place, there is a very clever view in the *Northern Tourist*, from the talented pencil of Mr Allom; nor is there a less clever view of the 'Depot,' at Hexham, or the place where we halted, than in Mr Blackmore's pleasing publication. We made for the 'Black Bull Inn'; bespeaking a chaise to conduct us to *Chesters*, as soon as we should have completed a circuit of the town, and seen the principal sights. Our kind friend, Mr Adamson, had furnished us with a letter to the Rev Mr Airy, a gentleman well versed in all *Hexhamite* antiquities. He attended us to the *Abbey Church*, of which little more than the transept and choir are left, deserving especial notice. The transept, one hundred and fifty-six feet in length, has a noble aspect. The choir, about seventy feet only in length, is in the chaste style of early English architecture towards the end of the thirteenth century; resembling, both in style and size, that of Southwell Minster. It is however defaced – rather than dignified, as intended by its donor – by a gallery of deal pews. Many things about it demanded a more leisurely survey; and the tomb or shrine of *Prior Richard*, and an almost obliterated *Dance of Death*, served to arrest our attention for a considerable time. A good deal of the earlier portion of the twelfth century is yet left to refresh and delight the eye of the antiquary; and the modern architect, even though he be the favourite of the Church Commissioners, may be astonished to learn that the walls of the side aisles of the choir are *ten feet thick*. The pigmy ecclesiastical structures of the present day shrink into insignificance before these mighty masses of ancient brick and stone. Within the precincts of the church-yard, and within little more than a foot of the surface of the earth, was found, some three years ago, an earthen vessel, containing not fewer than three thousand *stycas*, or Saxon coins, which have been made known to the public by the archaeological pen of Mr Adamson.

From the church we proceeded to an old tower near the market-place, where some precious monuments are preserved, to pay our respects to Mr Bell, the town-clerk; a gentleman who appeared to be embedded in these faded membraneous evidences of the olden times. His very countenance and costume seemed to belong to the Hexham-battle period. The whole picture was in fine keeping; and I felt truly sensible of his civilities and attention … I should think this tower could not be older than the reign of Edward III. In our way thither, or rather on immediately quitting the Abbey Church, Mr Airy conducted us to what had been the old, but now the new, GRAMMAR SCHOOL – in which the church registers are kept …

I do not remember to have seen a market-place – even in any town of Normandy – exhibit a more lively picture than did this of Hexham, on the day of our visit. Rival vendors, pitted against each other, in carts, made the air ring with their vociferations. Hardware glittered here; crockery was spread out there: hats maintained a sable phalanx in a third place; while, in a fourth, a stentorian orator appeared to be almost splitting his cheeks, as well as bursting his lungs, in an elaborate eulogy upon a pair of corduroy small-clothes. The audience, collected in pretty good numbers, seemed to look on in silent wonder; but no purchase was made during my observation of this motley scene. There was a man in a cart, hard by, who ever and anon kept thrusting forward knives, razors, hatchets and axes; displaying an agility, and an escape from accident, in a manner that perfectly astonished me. He should be hired for Astley's or Sadler's Wells. A bell tolled the hour of one, and every vendor and orator became silent – at his dinner-meal.

A chaise, of somewhat stubborn construction, and a pair of horses that might have carried their own plough at the tail of the chaise, brought us in good time to CHESTERS, the seat of William Clayton, Esq.

A postcard of Market Day in the 1950s.

A Letter to Edwin Chadwick, 1852
from Robert Rawlinson (Health Inspector)

I found the town in a state of ferment as to the inquiry, the bell-man was perambulating the streets summonsing the ratepayers to a meeting to oppose the inquiry. This was repeated during the evening, one of the meetings being for the evening, the others for the morning. Several of the promoters called in upon me during the evening, evidently fearing the morning's meeting. I explained the Act to them, as the most absurd statements had been published and were believed. I learned that the leader of the opponents was a Local Solicitor. The promoters were most anxious to learn what course I should take, as they feared to come forward and support the measure in public, that is they would attend the meeting but wished to avoid taking an active part in the proceedings. I told them this was exactly the course I desired they should take – namely – let the opposition have all the talking to themselves, and so leave them to me as I was quite sure out of their own evidence I could convict, if not convince them. The inquiry had to be adjourned to a large room as there was a full and rather formidable attendance. The day being wet many workmen were there. I commenced the inquiry by a short statement of the proceedings which had brought me down – and then glanced rapidly over the powers contained in the Act – taking up one by one the objections which I had been informed the promoters of the opposition had made. I then requested any persons having evidence either for or against to come forward and tender it. The opponents entered most resolutely into the arena, declaring that Hexham was well supplied with water; and was, in all other respects, a perfect town. I inquired for the return of the mortality, and found that, for the last seven years, it was actually some 29 in the thousand, but with 'cooked' returns it was 24 in the thousand. I then called the Medical Officers and the Relieving Officers and soon got amongst causes of fever, small-pox, and excessive money relief. I then traced disease to crowded room tenements, undrained streets, lanes, courts and crowded yards, foul middens, privies and cesspools. The water I found was deficient in quantity and most objectionable in quality, dead dogs having to be lifted out of the reservoir. And though the opposition fought stoutly they were obliged publicly to acknowledge that improvement was needed – they, however, dreaded the General Board, and the expense. I then explained the constitution of the Board and stated that their powers would be used to instruct, protect, and to check extravagant expenditure. By this time the eagerness of the opponents had somewhat subsided, the body of the meeting had come partially round, and so I entered into an examination of the promoters who came willingly forward. At the termination of the inquiry several of the opponents came forward and stated that I had removed their objections and they wished the Act could be applied immediately.

Today I have inspected the town – and have found it as bad as any place I ever saw. I have had at least twenty gentlemen with me all day although it has rained most of the time. The town is old, and in as bad a condition as Whitehaven, and I don't know that I can say anything worse of it. I am staying at the best Hotel in the town, but there is no watercloset, only a filthy privy at some distance – the way to it being past the kitchen. I have just been out in the dark and rain blundering and found someone in the place.

I have inspected the sources of the present water supply, and find that the water is taken from an open brook, filthy and muddy in wet weather, and filthy and bright in dry weather. In the same districts I have found; or rather, been shewn, springs – pure and soft – and at a sufficient elevation, to give 150 foot pressure in the town – and in abundance for the whole population. The existing springs will be added to if requisite by deep drainage. Most complete waterworks might be formed at a cheap cost. And the town may be sewered and drained for nothing, as a Nursery Man adjoining has stated that he will give £100 a year for the refuse, if it is all collected by drains. There are many acres of market gardens and nursery grounds within reach of the outlet sewer and more than £100 a year will be obtained.

Since the inspection today I have had parties from both sides with me, the opponents trying to explain away their opposition; the promoters to furnish information; and, at times, I have had nine or ten gentlemen at once, belonging to both parties. The leader of the opposition has made me a present of some Anglo-Saxon coins – called Stycus, which were found in Hexham Church Yard.

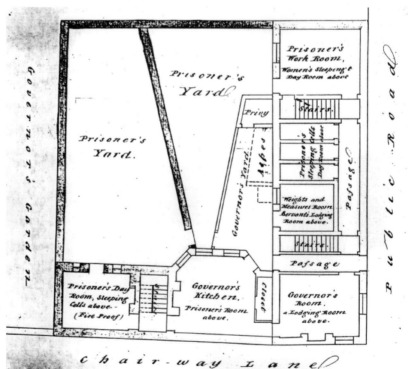

A plan of the House of Correction at Hexham, 1839.

The Town Hall and Corn Exchange, Beaumont Street. Built in 1865-66, it is now the Queen's Hall Library and Arts Centre. It was saved from demolition in 1980 by joint action of the District and County Councils.

A multiple view postcard showing the exterior and interior of the Queen's Hall.

'WIBSON'

HEXHAM'S 'PEOPLE'S POET'

WILFRID WILSON GIBSON (1878-1962)

Heather land and bent-land,
Black land and white,
God bring me to Northumberland,
The land of my delight.

Land of singing waters,
And winds from off the sea,
God bring me to Northumberland,
The land where I would be.

Heather land and bent-land,
And valleys rich with corn,
God bring me to Northumberland,
The land where I was born.

Wilfrid Gibson, author of poems like 'Flannan Isle', 'The Ice Cart', and 'The Drover's Road', was born in Battle Hill, Hexham, on 2nd October 1878, the son of a Fore Street chemist. He grew up under the guidance of an elder sister who was responsible for much of his education. Not much is known about his early years except for a distinct gift for language and a desire to be a poet. His first published poem appeared in *The Spectator* in 1897 and his first book of poetry was published at the age of 24 and entitled *The Golden Helm*. Similarly romantic was his next book, *Urlyn the Harper*, published two years later. This was followed, in 1907, by *Stonefields* which depicted the strength and atmosphere of Northumberland and the Borders, and then *Daily Bread*, issued in 1910, which went into a third printing, partly because of its down-to-earth style proving that there was a market for poems on everyday life which people could relate to. Gibson had ceased writing pseudo-Tennysonian verse and had begun to write realistic poetry in which he attempted to reflect the speech of ordinary people, based on events stemming from everyday life in Northumberland and elsewhere. He was also a reluctant playwright whose verse dialogues were frequently performed. His play *Womankind* was performed in Birmingham and Glasgow, as well as at the Chicago Little Theatre. However, he lacked real dramatic gift and found the conventions of theatre distasteful to a man who was a recluse by temperament.

He was not without his critics, like the poet Edward Thomas who said in 1906 that: 'Wilfrid Wilson Gibson had long ago swamped his

A studio portrait of Gibson taken at Hunter's Studios, Fore Street.

small delightful gift by his abundance. He is essentially a minor poet in the bad sense, for he is continually treating subjects poetically, writing about things instead of creating them.' Of Gibson's later verse narratives, Thomas was equally scathing: 'Gibson has merely been embellishing what would have been more effective as pieces of rough prose. The verse has added nothing except unreality, not even brevity.'

Gibson first left the middle-class security of his home in Hexham in 1907 to reside briefly in Glasgow where he was accepted into literary society as a hard up but genteel poet. He reviewed books for the *Glasgow Herald*.

In the summer of 1912, with 10 published volumes to his credit, Gibson finally left Hexham for London to broaden his literary horizons and never returned to his native town, except for very occasional visits. He was known by editors John Middleton Murry and Katherine Mansfield as a contributor to the magazine Rhythm and they found a cheap room in the city, above the 'Poetry Bookshop', for the penniless poet who worked for a while as a social worker in the East End.

Impressed by Gibson's 'singular integrity', the literary patron Edward Marsh published him in *Georgian Poetry* and also appointed him assistant editor of *Rhythm*.

Gibson moved to Dymock in Gloucestershire in 1913 to join a group of poets and his new bride, Geraldine Townshend (secretary of poet Harold Munro of the Poetry Bookshop in London), who he had married in Dublin, went with him. One of the Dymock Poets, the American Robert Frost, said of Gibson that: 'he is much talked of in America at the present time. He's just one of the plain folks with none of the marks of the literary poseur about him'. Gibson's friend, the poet Rupert Brooke, affectionately nicknamed him 'Wibson' and made him one of his heirs. Gibson was turned down by the Army because of his shaky health and poor eyesight but was recruited to the war effort in 1917 when he served as a clerical worker in the Army Service Corps at Sydenham, near London. Shortly beforehand, he had embarked upon a successful reading tour of America. His son Michael was born in 1918.

Gibson always belittled his own work. Speaking about his small volume Battle, which contained 32 poems about the war, he said: 'I had to publish it as I felt I must make my little protest, however feeble and ineffectual – so don't be too hard on me.'

In war and in peace, he tried to capture the lives of ordinary people and he acquired a reputation as a poet who identified with the urban poor and who understood the harshness of the lives of working people, what he called 'the heartbreak in the heart of things'.

'Wibson' continued to publish a selection of poems every two years or so until 1950 and he still went on reading and lecturing tours around Britain, despite money problems and the aches and pains of rheumatism and fibrositis. But his work declined greatly in popularity and is scarcely known today, though it was included in Philip Larkin's *Oxford Book of 20th Century Verse*.

He died at Virginia Water in Surrey in a nursing home on 26th May

1962, aged 83. He had written to Robert Frost in 1939 that: 'I am one of those unlucky writers whose books have predeceased him.'

Yet, as Gibson said himself, 'We shall always have poets while we have lovers.' To this extent, his poetry lives on in 'The Heart Of All England'. On 11th November (Armistice Day) 1985 a slate stone was unveiled in Westminster Abbey commemorating sixteen Great War poets, including the name of Wilfrid Gibson.

Below is the inscription on the north side of the Market Cross and Fountain. N.B. 'Wilfrid' misspelt on Memorial!

O YOU WHO DRINK MY COOLING WATERS CLEAR
FORGET NOT THE FAR HILLS FROM WHENCE THEY FLOW
WHERE OVER FELL AND MOORLAND YEAR BY YEAR
SPRING SUMMER AUTUMN WINTER COME AND GO
WITH SHOWERING SUN AND RAIN AND STORM AND SNOW
WHERE OVER THE GREEN BENTS FOREVER BLOW
THE FOUR FREE WINDS OF HEAVEN; WHERE TIME FALLS

IN SOLITARY PLACES CALM AND SLOW.
WHERE PIPES THE CURLEW AND THE PLOVER CALLS,
BENEATH THE OPEN SKY MY WATERS SPRING
BENEATH THE CLEAR SKY WELLING FAIR AND SWEET,
A DRAUGHT OF COOLNESS FOR YOUR THIRST TO BRING,
A SOUND OF COOLNESS IN THE BUSY STREET.

WILFRED WILSON GIBSON   HEXHAM FEB-1901

The unveiling of a commemorative plaque to Gibson by Councillor J.M. Pescott, Mayor of Hexham, 5th October 1978.

Market Cross And Fountain, 1901

The south side of the Market Cross and Fountain bears the following inscription:

> FOR THE COMMON GOOD
> PLACED HERE
> NEAR THE SITE OF THE OLD MARKET PANT
> IN THE 64TH YEAR OF THE REIGN OF
> QUEEN VICTORIA
> AND THE FIRST OF
> KING EDWARD THE VII
> A.D. 1901.

On the west side are the Arms of Hexham Priory and on the east side the Arms of Northumberland.

Hexham Market Cross and Fountain was officially opened on 28th August 1901. The Fountain was erected in memory of Willam Angus Temperley by the members of his family, and affixed to its base are four copper plates. The reason the Fountain has no plaque indicating the connection with the Temperley family is that W.A. Temperley made it clear that he and the family did not wish there to be one. The original

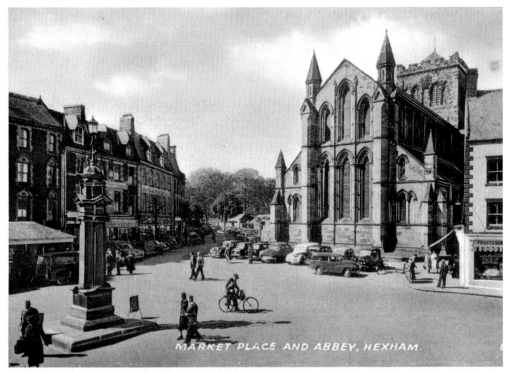

The fountain in the Market Place in the early 1950s.

structure had 4 gas lights on ornamental standards. Immediately below the dome are 8 carvings: east face – cross keys with a crown above for the Archbishop of York; south east – 3 lions rampant guardant for England; south – a cross bearing 4 lions rampant for the Bishop of Durham; south west – St Andrew's cross for Hexham; west – 3 castles with a cross above for the Bishop of Newcastle; north west – the Irish harp for Ireland; north – a cross with a mitre for the Bishop of Carlisle; north east – a lion rampant for Scotland.

On the south east pilaster the rose for England is clear – the south west bears a harp and leeks; at the top of the north west pilaster, 1901 can just be made out; at the top of the north east pilaster is E V11, below it a thistle.

The Fountain in 2002.

RACING INTO THE HISTORY BOOKS

Hexham Races, 1904.

Horse racing in Hexham dates back to the eighteenth century when meetings were documented on Tyne Green during the 1720s.

Some form of flat racing took place from time to time at the Yarridge course from the late 1790s. Today's facilities are a long way removed from the few timber huts created in the late nineteenth century.

Steeplechasing did not appear in Northumberland until 1840 when a meeting was held at Morpeth. By the early 1860s, racing had become established at Wark and according to local reports the 1865 meeting there saw the local rail station barely able to cope with the huge crowds, including the Marquess of Queensberry and the High Sheriff of Northumberland, who were entertained between races by the Acomb Band and a band from Germany. No beer was allowed – only spirits!

The success of the meeting enabled the committee to build a grandstand and, for the next three years, Wark flourished, with prize money reaching as much as £70 for the winners of principal races.

The impact of Wark's success was felt at Hexham's Yarridge course. During the 1870s, things reached crisis-point – with no permanent buildings, only tents and marquees for shelter, crowds dwindled and the gates at Hexham Racecourse were closed in 1880 for a period of 10 years.

A day at the Races.

In the early months of 1890, a group of local leading-lights decided that racing should be revived at Yarridge and turned to businessman Charles William Chipchase Henderson ('CWC') who had recently sold his company Durham Carpets and moved to the Tynedale area. He took responsibility for the entire course management and put a substantial amount of his own money into it.

Racing began again later in 1890 as a private venture under National Hunt rules over an all-pasture course and, within a year, two permanent wooden buildings were erected for weighing and changing rooms, and a fenced paddock was created. Things went from strength to strength so much so that a 1893 fixture was described as like 'Gosforth Park on Plate Day'.

Come 1907, and 'CWC' bought the racecourse land himself and began a series of improvements, including planting the unique beech hedge wings at each steeplechase fence which remain to this day. The same year the Town and Trades of Hexham presented the Heart of All England Cup for the steeplechase of the same name, which has been running ever since in early May.

Charles Henderson died in 1914 and the ownership of Yarridge was passed on to his son Stephen.

The War and the Depression seriously affected the racecourse and in 1926 Stephen Henderson turned it into a limited company with the Hendersons having a controlling share, which they retain to this day.

Racing survived and began to flourish again in the 1930s when

Racing At Yarridge

further additions were made to the paddock, public rooms, and grandstand. But the outbreak of war in 1939 meant a further cessation of racing and the course and buildings were requisitioned by the War Department for use as an ammunition dump.

Accountant Wiiliam Patterson steered the company through the war and, when the course was released by the Ministry of Defence, racing commenced anew with the Whitsun meeting of 1946, this time under the direction of C.D. 'Kit' Patterson, William's son. 'Kit' controlled things for the next 40 years.

There were periods during the '50s and '60s when attendances slumped and this was particularly the case after the legalising of betting shops in 1962. However, with financial help from the then Betting Levy Board, racing at Hexham kept on going.

In 1986, almost 100 years after the revival of racing by C.W.C. Henderson, his great grandson Charles Enderby returned to the family home after a career in the Army. He took over as Clerk of the Course and later succeeded 'Kit' Patterson as Managing Director of the Hexham Steeplechase Company.

In 1990, the Henderson Building was opened, replacing some of the old structures to provide a new weighing room, changing rooms, viewing areas, medical and photographic facilities, and a new dining area. Two years later, a sponsorship deal with the Federation Brewery saw the introduction of hospitality boxes in the Buchanan Suite.

During 1994, the Haydon Hunt was given permission to construct a pont-to-point course inside the steeplechase track.

Bookie's Suit

In return
for your soiled cash,
he gives you scraps
of paper that fly
across these hard-earned
        fields of Yarridge,
through history.

Keith Armstrong, Year of the Artist poet-in-residence, Hexham Races, 2000.

Right: Leading lights at Hexham Racecourse: C.W.C. Henderson (left) and Sir Loftus Bates.

More recently, a lake was created in the centre of the course to ensure a supply of water to improve the going in summer. The lake has become a sanctuary for wild birds, such as the curlew.

In May 1998, an extension to the Henderson Building was opened. The 'Ramshaw Stand' is named after the chairman of the Federation Brewery and offers a range of catering facilities. A new Tote betting shop was opened in 1999 by the Princess Royal.

(With acknowledgements to 'Curlew', racing correspondent of the *Hexham Courant*.)

From 'Lady Jockey, Hexham Races'

I will ride
forever
breathing ecstatically;
an animal love
in my lungs;
and the smell
of a bold Northumberland
scenting
my bracing hair.

Keith Armstrong

Racing Memories

Hexham Races May meeting, 1899.

The Races, 1904.

Vale Of Tyne

Vale of Tyne! sweet spring returning
Soon will deck thy groves again:
When the lark awakes the morning
With its sweet and soothing strain;
When the trees their buds are showing,
And the bright spring-flowers are glowing
Where the zephyrs softly blowing,
Scatter verdure on the plain.

Soon again shall beauteous summer
Clothe the fruitful fields with green,
Scattering pleasant odours from her,
Strewing flowers to deck the scene;
When the sunshine gilds the river,
Whose soft murmur ceases never,
Flowing down thy bosom ever,
Those enamell'd banks between.

On the hill of Yarridge standing,
In the summer twilight pale,
With enraptured gaze commanding
All the beauties of the vale;
Smiling fields are spread before us,
Blithesome larks are singing o'er us;
And the woodlands join in chorus,
Sweet as songs of nightingale.

See the landscape far extending,
Verdant lawns and meadows gay,
Till the ambient sky seems blending
With the blue hills far away;
See the quiet homesteads near ye,
Once I thought them dull and dreary,
Now of aimless wandering weary,
Glad, contented I can stay.

George Chatt

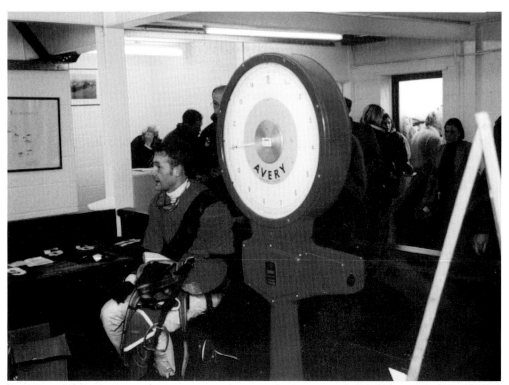

Two modern views of Hexham Races.

WORDS ON HEXHAM

The exterior and interior of the Forum, *circa* 1939 – showing one of the most popular films of all-time, *Gone With The Wind*.

Hexham Tans

'Hides lifted from a lime-pit were soaked for days, scraped and 'bated' in solutions of dog excrement and ground bark before hanging up to dry.'

You ancient company
of skinners and glovers,
you gossiping crafts.

You hatters and tanners,
leather-dressers and cutters,
we can hear you and sniff you in Hexham's dank lanes.

You clockmakers and bookbinders,
pipemakers and joiners,
we touch your worksore hands.

You shoemakers and collarmakers,
weavers and saddlers,
we bear your burdens and your smiles.

You dressmakers,
ropeworkers,
cabinetmakers
basketmakers.
Tinsmiths and
millwrights,
butchers and
engravers.

You 1,000 sewing women in your homes,
you bakers and tapestry-makers,
you've led us here –

we worship you,
we drink your sweat.

Keith Armstrong

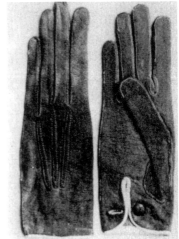

Hexham Tans.

Hexham Proverbs
Collected by M.A. Denham, 1854

1. *Hexham Measure; up-heaped, pressed down, and running over!*

Some of the Dry Measures used at Hexham did not correspond with those of the same name in general use in the North of England. Thus, what is called a *Ball* of corn in Hexham contains four Winchester bushels, the customary number, in other places, being only two.

2. *He comes fra' Hexham Green, and that's ten miles ayont Hell.*

Refers to Tyne Green where the fairs used to be held.

3. *Every one to their ain hand, like the Pipers of Hexham.*

To pipe for one's own hand, is to pipe for any party who will employ one, without knowing or recking whether they be friend or foe. Or, in other words – *To pipe for those who pay one best.*

4. *Hexham, where they knee-band lops and put spectacles upon blind spiders.*

A derisive proverb occasionally applied to other places.

5. *Silly-good-natured, like a Hexham goose; bid him sit down, and he will lie down.*

6. *A Hexham Goose.*

Natives of Hexham are so called collectively. During heavy snow storms people used to say – 'The country gowks are ploating their Geese, and sending the feathers to Hexham.'

7. *He's getten up the lang stairs.*

A Hexham saying, parallel with that of Newcastle – *He's getten into limbo; up the nineteen steps,* i.e. into prison.

The Hexhamshire Lass

Its hey for the buff and the blue,
Hey for the cap and the feather;
Hey for the bonny lassie true,
That lives in Hexhamshire.

Thro' by the Saiby Syke,
And o'er the moss and the mire,
I'll go to see my lass,
Who lives in Hexhamshire.

Her father lov'd her well,
Her mother lov'd her better;
I love the lass mysel',
But, alas! I cannot get her.
Thro' by, &c.

Oh, this love, this love!
Of this love I am weary!
Sleep I can get none,
For thinking on my deary!
Thro' by, &c.

My heart is like to break,
My bosom is on fire;
So well I love the lass
That lives in Hexhamshire.
Thro' by, &c.

Her petticoat is silk,
And plaited round with siller;
Her shoes are tied with tape,
She'll wait 'til I go till her.
Thro' by, &c.

Were I where I would be,
I would be beside her;
But here a while I must be,
Whatever may betide her.
Thro' by, &c.

Hey for the thick and the thin,
Hey for the mud and the mire;
And hey for the bonny lass
That lives in Hexhamshire.
Thro' by, &c.

Account of a stay in Hexham's White Horse Inn, *circa* 1853

by William Bell Scott

Midway between the eastern and western shores of our hard-working
island I found myself in the old-fashioned, sleepy town of Hexham, and
settled down in a small apartment in the half-timbered hostelry called
the White Horse. This apartment was over the porch, and the front of it
was one continuous narrow casement with a long bunker seat under it,
looking out on the quiet Market-place and great church, once a
Cathedral, partly destroyed by the Scotch, but still large enough for all
the inhabitants of the town. This long window, with the casements
opened, and this Market-place seen without, was my subject,
and the landlady's daughter posed to me at full length on the window-
seat knitting. I entered into the homely daily life of the narrow circle,
and soon began to know the bellman and the beadle, the apothecary
and the mercer, and to recognize the domestic damsels, each one at her
regular moment coming for the daily water to the fountain. Then the
sun was always shining, my casement was always open, the pigeons
and the jackdaw, the 'familiar' – a quite innocent one – of the Market-
place, sat on the sill looking at me in their sidelong bird fashion. Every
quarter of an hour the great clock of the cathedral chimed soberly –
one for the quarter, two for the half, and so on till it struck the hour. I
begun to think it said this, accenting the first word of each line:

> Now must I show my power –
> Here it surely comes once more –
> Now must I declare the hour –
> Day and night, and o'er and o'er.

At noon, before the last stroke of the bell had ceased to vibrate, the
clatter of wooden shoes and the hubbub of children's voices showed
that the school had been opened. Into the wide paved space they
tumbled, Esaus and Ishmaels starting to fight over the horse-trough,
splashing the water about, and pairs of good Davids and Jonathans
keeping their arms round each other's necks. The tall maiden Isabell,
my model, by and by disappeared to cook my dinner and to eat her
own, and when my hour came I very often found a roasted duckling
before my solitary plate.

This hostelry was scarcely ever disturbed by traveller, except on one
day, the market-day of the week, yet the landlady, who had her cares,
having lost everything sixteen years before, when her son was banished
for forgery, cheerfully said the world had been very good to her; she
had now something in the bank of her own again, her son was now a
prosperous man, and she was looking for his return.

*The artist William Bell Scott painted the murals at Wallington Hall
depicting scenes from Northumbrian history.*

Lines Written To Celebrate The Opening Of The Newcastle And Carlisle Railway From Hexham To Haydon Bridge 28th June 1836

Have you heard what a day we have had.
Had you seen but the sights we have seen,
'Twould have made every one of you glad,
As it made all that saw it, I ween
From Blaydon an engine did come
With its long train of beauty and worth,
While a band with a pond'rous big drum,
Its music pour'd pleasantly forth.

The streamers all waved in the air,
The Hexham bells rung many a peel,
Some thousands assembled there were,
And pleasure each bosom did feel.
The young and the aged were there,
The rich and the poor in a line,
The whole cavalcade, I declare,
Wan by every one said to be fine.

The two trains looked beautiful too,
While the streamers and flags waved along,
The whole was most pleasant to view,
And furnished a theme for a song,
When we approached fam'd Haydon Bridge,
Great numbers of people were there,
On the plains or on the hill ridge,
Some hundreds or thousands there were.

After four the trains start anew,
And now they increased in their speed,
The managers must have their due,
They deserved thanks and praises indeed;
All their duty did there, I declare,
And all gave them credit that day,
To Hexham all came hale and fair,
And all as they like took their way.

Matthew Wilson

Matthew Wilson was the 'local poet laureate'. A Liberal and supporter of the 1832 Reform Bill, he made a great speech in the town's Moot Hall, when he collapsed into 'bursts of laughter at the jokes he passed upon the tyrant Tories'. He was also a local preacher and keeper of the Half Moon Inn, hence his description, by the *Newcastle Journal*, as: 'The Reverend Landlord of the split dish.' He wrote verse on any striking event and sold his poems at the 'small charge of one penny'.

OPENING OF HEXHAM RAILWAY STATION.

This view of Hexham depot was published in 1836 and was drawn by the well-known Newcastle artist J.W. Carmichael.

HEXHAM 7

NEWCASTLE & CARLISLE RAILWAY.

NOTICE.

On or about the 2nd June Instant, TWO SACKS OF FLOUR were MISSING from the Hexham Station, and have not since been found, they are supposed to have been taken away by mistake; whoever will give such information to Mr. DIXON, at the Station, as will lead to the recovery of the same, will be handsomely rewarded.

BY ORDER,

JOHN ADAMSON,
CLERK TO THE COMPANY.

Railway Office, Forth, Newcastle,
June 25, 1847.

PRINTED AT THE GUARDIAN OFFICE, GRAINGER STREET, NEWCASTLE.

A Newcastle & Carlisle Railway notice from 1847.

Hexham Women's Own

One lovely day, the third of May,
I went to Hexham town,
A noted place for means of grace,
A place of great renown.
I went to speak and some friends seek,
Some I had never known.
I'm glad to say 'twas meeting day
With Hexham Women's Own.

Both young and old, as good as gold,
Came to the meeting there.
When I sat down that afternoon
I saw some at me stare.
They thought that I was looking shy,
An old man all alone,
But I kept bright and did recite
To Hexham Women's Own.

After a while there was a smile
On nearly every face;
They seemed so glad, and none were sad
Within the meeting-place.
Hearts filled with joy without alloy,
This was so plainly shown.
This is all true, I'm telling you,
At Hexham Women's Own.

Sisters, be true, there's work for you;
And let your lights all shine,
And everyone keep pressing on.
Don't let your work decline.
The Master's voice bids you rejoice;
You shall not walk alone
If in His ways you spend your days
With Hexham Women's Own.

Keep near the Cross, you shall not lose,
But gain a mansion fair,
And join the band in that bright land
Where there's no grief or care.
Christ said one day, 'I am the way
That leadeth to God's throne.'
Be good and true, His ways pursue,
All Hexham Women's Own.

May blessings flow where'er you go,
And may you faithful be
To Him who says, 'Walk in My ways.'
The heavenly land you'll see.
Some day we'll meet at Jesu's feet,
And reap what we have sown.
Won't this be grand when there we stand
With Hexham Women's Own?

T. Campbell
(from *Tyneside Recitations,* 1928*)*

Gathering Nuts

by Thomas Spence (1750-1814)

In order to show how far we are cut off from the rights of Nature; and reduced to a more contemptible state than the Brutes, I will relate an affair I had with a Forester in a Wood near Hexham alone by myself a gathering of Nuts, the Forester popped through the Bushes upon me, and asking what I did there, I answered gathering Nuts: Gathering Nuts! said he, and dare you say so? Yes, said I, why not? Would you question a Monkey, or a Squirrel, about such a Business? And am I to be treated as inferior to one of those Creatures? Or have I a less right? But who are you, continued I, that thus take upon you to interrupt me? I'll let you know that, said he when I lay you fast for trespassing here. Indeed! answered I. But how can I trespass here where no Man ever planted or cultivated, for these Nuts are the spontaneous Gifts of Nature ordained alike for the Sustenance of Man and Beast, that choose to gather them, and therefore they are common. I tell you, said he, this Wood is no Common. It belongs to the Duke of Portland. Oh! My service to the Duke of Portland, said I, Nature knows no more of him than of me. Therefore, as in Nature's storehouse the Rule is, 'First come, first served,' so the Duke of Portland must look sharp if he wants any Nuts. But in the name of Seriousness, continued, must not one's privileges be very great in a country where we dare not pluck a Hazel Nut? Is this an Englishman's Birthright? Is it for this we are called upon to serve in the Militia, to defend this Wood, and this Country, against the Enemy?

What must I say to the French, if they come? If they jeeringly ask me what I am fighting for? Must I tell them for my Country? For my dear Country in which I dare not pluck a Nut? Would not they laugh at me? Yes. And do you think I would bear it? No: Certainly I would not. I would throw down my Musket saying let such as the Duke of Portland, who claim the Country, fight for it, for I am but a stranger and sojourner, and have neither Part nor Lot amongst them.

This reasoning had such an effect on the Forester that he told me to gather as many Nuts as I pleased.

Seal Walk.

Ring Your Bells

Hexham,
let me shake your townsfolk by the hand,
as I finger the shelves of Northumberland.
Over centuries, the blood has darted
through the arteries of the brave faint-hearted;
hands have caressed and hands have waved,
hands have destroyed and bodies saved.

Hexham,
in my glove I hold your history,
I squeeze the tears from all your mystery.
Across the bridge, the trades have fled,
fingerprinted the river-bed.
Tools have hammered and tools have shaped,
tools have made and bodies raped.

Hexham,
maker of many a thousand gloves,
your people mad as hatters' loves,
ring your bells
and wring your hands
and hope that Wilfrid understands.

Keith Armstrong

IMAGES OF OLD HEXHAM

Fore Street, pre 1919.

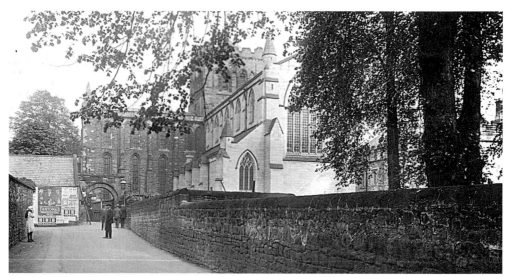

A view of the Abbey from around 1924. The old vicarage is on the left.

A view of the Abbey with the bowling green in the foreground.

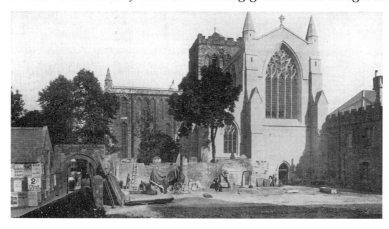

Completition of new nave at the, 1908.

The Bandstand, Abbey Grounds. It was presented by Henry Bell, Wool Merchant in 1912.

The Queen came to Hexham on 1st July 1974 to a Service of Thanksgiving for the preservation of the Abbey throughout the past 1,300 years since its foundation. She is accompanied here by the Lord Bishop of Newcastle, the Right Reverend Ronald Bowlby, and the Rector of Hexham, the Reverend Rowland Lemmon.

A busy scene in the Market Place in the 1950s.

Stalls on Market Day.

A view of Hexham from the Nurseries, *circa* 1902.

Medieval bridge, in Hexham House grounds, with early nineteenth century eye-catching parapet.

Cattle Market from Battle Hill, 1907.

Battle Hill in the 1920s.

Battle Hill – with J.R. Denton's newsagents on the left. Note the several signs for cigarettes.

Horse and hounds in Battle Hill. Note the North East Railway Co horse and cart to the left.

H.P. Rose – Tailor & constumier, hosier & outfitter – No 5 Battle Hill, 1914. The building is now incorporated into the National Westminster Bank.

A trade postcard for a 'potato merchant, fruiter and florist' in Priestpopple. 'Noted for select quality'.

A view of Priestpopple from the east towards Cattle Market in the 1920s.

A 1950s view showing the pedestrian crossing in Priestpopple.

Cattle Market from Battle Hill.

The Red Lamp Hotel, Fore Street,
around 1907.

A view of Fore Street from the top of
the Midland Bank in the early 1950s.

A crowd gathers for the photographer in St Mary's Chare around 1902. Could the flags and bunting be out for the Coronation of Edward VII?

The entrance to St Mary's Chare from Old Church.

Porteous Thomson and H.W. Gillies, Ironmonger, Market Place. Are the flags and bunting out this time for the Coronation of George V in 1911?

'Ginky' – real name Dodd who lived in the Prior Terrace area. His first words every morning were: 'Whee's Deed?' It is said he attended every funeral for miles.

Priestpopple from the Cattle Market, 1890s.

Battle Hill around 1914. The postcard is marked with a cross and the sender of this card has written: 'Cross is where I live the top of the house.'

Tynedale Hydropathic Mansion. A hydropath establishment, opened in 1879, was built alongside Westfield House; the architect was Mr Newcombe of Newcastle. The grounds extended to about 20

acres and it could receive upwards of 100 visitors. It did not meet with the success the promoters anticipated, went into liquidation and was sold by auction in 1886. In 1896 it was offering baths and Turkish baths to the outside public and a very large number of people spent their Christmas and New Year holidays at the Hydro. The Winter Gardens were erected in 1907. The 55-bedroom Hydro was sold in 1931 and Hexham Hydro (1932) Ltd was formed.

The Hydro was closed in 1939 to receive TB patients from Stannington Sanatorium, it never reopened as a hotel. A mobile bakery was stationed in part of the Hydro in 1943 supplying RASC Supply Depots at Fenham Barracks, Newcastle and elsewhere. In 1950 the Northern Counties Training College of Cookery & Domestic Science, Newcastle, moved in. In 1962 the 'Hydro Girls' were followed by students from Ponteland Teacher Training College. The Winter Gardens had been kept in good condition through the 1950s by gardeners, with the plants and original cane furniture much as it had been before the war, but was allowed to deteriorate after the Teacher Training College moved in. The Hydro was acquired by Queen Elizabeth Grammar

School, by then in the adjoining site in Whetstone Bridge Road, in 1974 and in 1976 the reorganised QE High School with 1,300 pupils expanded into the Hydro Building.

The Winter Gardens. A postcard sent to South Shields in 1908.

The Convalescent Home around 1909. It was opened in 1893 and was used until its closure in 1937 after an epidemic of Septic Pneumonia.

The Seal Gates, Hencotes, pre 1908, showing the 1825 Scotch Church.

Laying the foundation stone for the Primitive Methodist Chapel, Whit Monday, 8th June 1908. The chapel in Beaumont Street was opened in 1909 and finally closed as a place of worship in 1957.

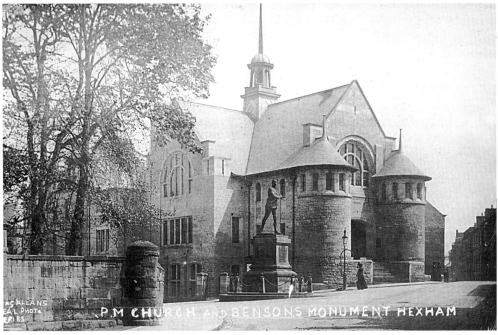

The Primitive Methodist Central Chapel with Benson's Monument, 1909. George Elliott Benson was born in 1861 and died in South Africa in 1901. The bronze statue by John Tweed recognises Lt Col Benson as a Hexham soldier hero.

Laying the foundation stone for the Abbey's new nave, St Peter's Day, 29th June 1907.

St Mary's Church, Hencotes.

The Old Gaol – Archbishop's Prison or Manor Office. Built in 1330, it now houses the Border History Museum.

The People's History

To receive a catalogue of our latest titles send a large SAE to:

The People's History
Suite 1
Byron House
Seaham Grange Business Park
Seaham
County Durham
SR7 0PY

www.thepeopleshistory.co.uk